100 IDEAS
FOR TEACHING MATHEMATICS

D0293946

CONTINUUM ONE HUNDREDS SERIES

OTHER MIKE OLLERTON TITLES

100 IDEAS
FOR TEACHING
MATHEMATICS

Mike Ollerton

continuum
LONDON • NEW YORK

Continuum International Publishing Group

The Tower Building   15 East 26th Street
11 York Road   New York
London   NY 10010
SE1 7NX

www.continuumbooks.com

British Library Cataloguing-in-Publication Data

A catalogue record for this book is available from the British Library.

ISBN: 0–8264–8481–6 (paperback)

Designed and typeset by Ben Cracknell Studios | Janice Mather

Printed and bound in Great Britain by MPG Books Ltd

*'useful, resourceful and inspiring . . .
this book is ideal for trainee teachers and NQTs'*

*'the ideas are designed to encourage and
invoke thinking among pupils'*

'a useful resource for teachers of mathematics'

*'this book not only provides inspirational activities
for the mathematics classroom but promotes a different
methodology of teaching mathematics, based on providing
students with meaningful, interesting, challenging and,
even, exciting experiences of discovering mathematical
truths for themselves'*

'accessible to both students and teachers alike'

CONTENTS

SECTION 2   Puzzles to NAG (Number, Algebra and Graphs) your students with

SECTION 3 **Puzzles to cause your students to *shape up***

SECTION 4 Puzzles to see how your students *measure up*

SECTION 5 **A few beer MATs, some glue and a lot of imagination**

SECTION 6 **SFGs, not perhaps as interesting as *The BFG* but nevertheless some giant-sized ideas for the classroom**

SECTION 7 **Ideas for budding data handlers**

ACKNOWLEDGEMENTS

I am indebted to Christina Parkinson (Continuum) for her encouragement and belief that I could put this collection of ideas together. Christina has remained consistently positive in her editorial comments, while ensuring I did not stray too far into a politico-educational minefield; this was no mean task!

I have also had some excellent feedback from the following reviewers: Dave Cubiss, Ian Green, Jo Jeffrey, Mark Leadbeater, Tom Pole and Lucy Slater. All these people offered me thoughts and suggestions that I used to clarify certain ideas and which I had wrongly assumed needed no further explanation.

I would also like to thank colleagues and students who suggested ideas to me, some of whom are acknowledged in the text . . . however there will be countless others whose ideas I have adopted and adapted yet who, in the mists of time, I am unable to identify.

While writing this book one of the Idries Shah 'stories' about Mulla Nasrudin came to mind. A paraphrase of the story goes as follows: Mulla Nasrudin is walking home from the market in his village and in his basket he has a delicious piece of liver which he is very much looking forward to cooking when he gets home. Unfortunately, on his way home a crow swoops down, snatches the piece of liver from Nasrudin's shopping basket and flies away high into the sky. Not to be daunted Nasrudin shakes his stick at the thieving bird and shouts '*You may have the liver . . . but you don't have the recipe!*'

In these days of prescribed curriculum and down-loadable lesson plans this story resonates for me, raising a concern I have about practice and pedagogy. I have long been concerned about 'experts' who offer advice and quick-tips for teachers without also engaging in pedagogical discussion, which is so important to underpin any ideas we take with us into classrooms and our continuing professional development. My concern is about how any teacher comes to 'own' the ideas they use in their classrooms. Ownership of teaching ideas is not about inventing the ideas in the first instance, neither is it about using another person's ideas without applying some critical analysis in the light of experience. Ownership is how a teacher adapts any ideas they pick up from various sources, meetings, conferences, resource books, etc. and makes them their own according to how they use them in their classrooms. When teachers are confident with the ideas they own they can help students become more independent, autonomous and responsible learners; I develop this below.

There is only one expert teacher in my classroom and that is me. The same goes for all other teachers. Of course we can develop our expertise and we can share pedagogic thoughts with other practitioners. However, when I come across a 'new' idea (well, new to me) I have to consider how I might weave it into my practice. I need to look at my recipe book containing my strategies and the resources I utilize and think about how best to cook with a new idea. This combination of ideas, strategies, resources and the unique teaching style form a large dose of pedagogy. The extra ingredients required are the rationale behind why anyone chooses to use an idea and the underlying reasons that cause us to choose to walk into classrooms and 'be' a teacher.

There are dangers of ideas being used as one-off activities. In the current orthodoxy of starters, middles and plenaries to lessons, which I have very many concerns about, I believe it is fundamentally important to construct starter tasks as the vehicle to develop students' deeper mathematical thinking. Starter tasks must be seen as something more than a strategy for settling a class or involving students in some form of mathematical gymnastics. 'Good' starter tasks are those which encourage development, where students are motivated to explore mathematical concepts and structures, where students can extend and enrich their mathematical thinking; a 'good' starter task might generate three or four weeks worth of lesson activity. It is important, therefore, to find tasks that have a shelf life longer than a single lesson and many of the ideas offered here are ripe for such development.

Returning to the issue of student independence, autonomy and responsibility the following encouragement, to help students develop such life skills, has been given by Ofsted as follows:

More schools need to employ strategies such as these to enable pupils to be more effective learners, for example to:
o become more autonomous and independent learners
o develop research and enquiry skills (and) . . .

o take more responsibility for their own progress and achievement.

Mathematics in the Secondary School, 2004

As students develop enquiry skills they become more autonomous and responsible, in short, they become more confident, more effective and wiser learners. As such I hope anybody who buys this book will consider how the ideas can be used and built upon to develop existing schemes of work and to deepen students' experience of mathematics and their expertise in being mathematicians.

Readers will not find any 'answers' in this book. This is because I am cautious about trying to focus too narrowly on where any idea might lead, even though some ideas offer more closed problems than others, for example Idea 52. Trying to help students see that while finding answers is important, there is value in engaging with the process and in recognizing that an answer need not be an end point but a staging post for asking other questions such as 'Why' and 'What happens if . . . ?' A comment I often make in classrooms is 'I'm not going to ask the questions and provide the answers', and so it is with this book.

Only a few Ideas are of my own 'invention'; the vast majority are adapted from various publications such as *Starting Points* (Tarquin) and *Points of Departure* (ATM) or have been suggested to me by colleagues and PGCE students who I have had the privilege to teach. Each idea I have either used in my practice or I have seen other teachers use with a measure of 'success'; they are, therefore, tried and tested. They are not, however, tried and tested in all other teachers' classrooms, certainly not in terms of how they are used or woven into schemes of work. For this reason it is important to recognize that the value of any idea depends upon the recipe an individual teacher uses to make the learning of mathematics accessible, intriguing, and palatable – happy cooking.

Mike Ollerton   XV

A number of number puzzles

A 100 square provides a rich environment for students to explore the number system and properties of numbers. While it is important for students to learn the value of flexibility, of seeing numbers emerge in different contexts and different formats, one useful format is to start with one at the bottom left hand corner and 100 at the top right-hand corner as in the diagram below. This is because the arrangement below is more consistent with graphs and vectors in the sense that moving to the right and up is a positive shift and moving to the left and down is a negative shift.

91	92	93	94	95	96	97	98	99	100
81	82	83	84	85	86	87	88	89	90
71	72	73	74	75	76	77	78	79	80
61	62	63	64	65	66	67	68	69	70
51	52	53	54	55	56	57	58	59	60
41	42	43	44	45	46	47	48	49	50
31	32	33	34	35	36	37	38	39	40
21	22	23	24	25	26	27	28	29	30
11	12	13	14	15	16	17	18	19	20
1	2	3	4	5	6	7	8	9	10

The first idea is to show the 100 square on a screen for approximately 10 seconds, turn the image off, then ask students to work out how many times the digit 1 appears in total. The intention here is for students to construct a mental picture of the 100 square and engage with the task above without having a copy in front of them.

For the following questions students may benefit by having a copy of the 100 square.

o   What does the first row of numbers add up to?

o   What do all the numbers in the second row total to?

o   What do all the numbers in the first three rows total to?

o   What do all the numbers in the first column total to?

o   What do all the numbers in the fourth column total to?

o   What do all the numbers in the diagonal from 1 to 100 total to?

o   What do all the numbers in the diagonal from 10 to 91 total to?

o   What do all the numbers in the whole 100 square total to?

These ideas are based upon shifts on the grid and one way to proceed is to show the whole class a single copy of the 100 square on a screen/board and ask students to write down some facts they know about the display of numbers. For example, students might write about how the numbers go vertically up by adding ten, or diagonally up to the right by adding 11. Students might be prompted to explore what pattern the multiples of three or the multiples of seven make, etc.

Having gathered students' responses, questions and possible tasks are likely to emerge quite naturally. Some typical questions I would certainly want to ask, with the display now switched off would be based upon 'Up', 'Down', 'Right' and 'Left' shifts, for example:

○ If I start at 7 and go one square up, where do I end up?
○ If I start at 64, go two squares down and one to the left, where do I end up?

Questions such as these will demand students engage in visualizing the grid.

The central idea here is for students to work with codes based upon the following shifts on the grid:
$U = +10$, $D = -10$, $R = +1$ and, $L = -1$.

Combinations of codes leads, for example, to
$UR = +11$, $DR = -9$ etc.

Having established this coding, questions might be posed such as: 57, **UUURR** = ?

A code such as 7, **DDR** will provide a context to work with negative numbers.

The coding system can be developed so 57, **UUURR** could be written as 57, $3U$, $2R$ = ? and students can make up and pose questions similar to these for each other to solve.

This might be an appropriate point to ask students to extend the grid in all four directions for two or three rows and columns, so they gain a sense that the system is continuous once the boundary of 100 squares is removed. In Idea 36, 100 square 3, I refer to this as the *extended grid.*

Trying to puzzle out the mathematics behind card tricks offers a rich vein of ideas for use in a mathematics classroom and having a number of 'tricks' up one's sleeve is useful; perhaps wheeling out a trick to add an element of intrigue into a lesson.

The following trick is taken from Martin Gardner's *Mathematics, Magic and Mystery* (Dover, 1956).

I saw it being used with great success by Phil Meek and David Rees at a PGCE Mathematics Activity Day (MAD).

The trick needs a deck of cards to be 'fixed' in the following way:

o On top of a deck of cards place eight cards so none of them are Aces.
o Now place the four Aces as card numbers nine, ten, eleven and twelve (from the top).
o Ask someone to call out any number between 10 and 20 (e.g. 17).
o Deal this number of cards off the top of the deck and place them face down; one, two, three . . . sixteen, seventeen. This means that the first card to be counted off the top of the deck becomes the card at the bottom of the pile of seventeen cards once they have been counted out. I shall refer to this as the 'new' pile.
o Next add together the digits of the number called out (1 + 7) and whatever this value is (i.e. 8), return this number of cards from the new pile back to the main deck; one, two, three . . . seven, eight.
o Take the next card on top of the (reduced) new pile and place this in an envelope.

Return all the cards in the new pile, that were initially dealt, back to the main deck and repeat the last four instructions three more times.

By the end of the trick you should have four cards in the envelope.

Ask someone to open the envelope and inside will be all four Aces . . . it's magic . . . well actually it is simple arithmetic, but who's counting? (And therein lies the solution!)

This is another idea which requires students to have access to packs of playing cards and was demonstrated to me by Tania Milnes, a PGCE student.

○ Turn over a card.
○ Whatever the face value of this card is, add further cards up to make 13.
○ Place these cards into a pile with all the cards face down.
○ Repeat this until all the cards have been used.
○ If there are any remaining cards (because a pile adding to 13 cannot be made) put these cards to one side.

For example, if a nine is turned over a further four cards are added to make a pile; the nine is then placed on top of pile 1 *face down*.

If the next card is a five, then eight more cards are counted from the pack and these, together with the five, make pile 2 (again the five is placed *face down* on top of this pile).

Continue this until all the cards have been used. There may be some remainder cards at the end (see below).

Court cards count as 11 for a Jack, 12 for a Queen and 13 for a King. So, if a King is turned over then no more cards are added to this particular pile because the total is already 13.

○ Ask someone to choose three of the piles and put these to one side.
○ Gather all the other piles together with the remainder cards into a 'stack'.
○ Ask someone else to choose one of the three piles and put this to one side.
○ Turn over the top card on each of the other two piles.
○ Add together the face value of these two cards and call this *f*.

o From the stack count out the same number of cards as the face value (f).

o Exclaim that the 'magic' number is ten and count a further ten cards from the stack.

The number of cards now left in the stack will be the value of the *face down* card on top of the chosen pile.

The question is, why does it work?

FIVES AND THREES

'Old fashioned' games based upon cards and dominoes, or simple pencil and paper games such as 'battleships', may not be seen as worthy competitors to high speed, wide-screen, wham-bam, crash-bang stimuli offered by the current generation of computer games. (No prejudice appearing in that sentence then!) In my experience, however, children also gain pleasure from simpler games requiring strategic and numerical thought.

Fives and threes is one such game and is played using dominoes, either with the set of 28 going up to double six or in some parts of the country a set of 55 going up to double nine.

The basic idea is to play dominoes by matching pairs of the same numbers together and adding together the values appearing at either end. Players score points according to whether this total is divisible by either five and/or three.

Doubles are placed vertically rather than horizontally. Below is the beginning of one such game:

Player A starts with and scores three points because $(5 + 4) \div 3 = 3$ (points).

If Player B adds the 6–5 domino to form the following arrangement:

 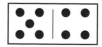

this gives a score of two because $(6 + 4) \div 5 = 2$ (points).

If Player A now plays the 4–3 this will give a score of three because $(6 + 3) \div 3 = 3$ (points)

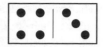

Scores are accumulated so Player A has now scored a total of six points.

If Player B now plays the double six this is placed 'vertically', as described above, so the two ends now total to 15 (i.e. 6 + 6 + 3). Player B scores eight points for making a total of 15 because 15 divides by both five and three, so $15 \div 5 = 3$ (points) and $15 \div 3 = 5$ (points).

The game continues and the winner is the person to score 121 points (or twice around a cribbage board).

The kind of task a teacher might engage a class with in order to help students understand the concept of divisor will be varied. Below I offer two approaches.

1   One teacher I worked with begins lessons on divisors by writing a number such as 20 on the board. She then asks individuals to call out another number and to each she offers one of two responses: '*Yes – I like that number*' or '*No – I don't like that number*'. Whether she says 'Yes' or 'No depends upon whether the numbers students call out are or are not a divisor of 20. The idea is for the students to determine why their teacher says 'Yes' or 'No'. This encourages a sense of puzzlement and creates a positive atmosphere.

2   Another approach is an idea offered to me by Emma Kearns, a former PGCE student I had the pleasure to work with.

The idea is based upon attributing each number with a certain amount of strips of paper. For example, eight has four strips of paper, folded as follows:

I	I	I	I	I	I	I	I
2		2		2		2	
4				4			
8							

This may help to explain why the number eight has four divisors, 1, 2, 4 and 8.

The question *How many strips of paper do other numbers have?* can now be posed.

As students begin to make sense of the concept of divisors there are several tasks which students can explore to practise their mental arithmetic and become more confident with their recall and knowledge of divisors. Further ideas appear on the following pages.

This task might be carried out in small groups and requires a simple resource of twenty or so pieces of card, each group being given a random selection of numbers between 1 and 100.

Each number is then written on a separate piece of card and the space underneath each number is left blank for students to fill in. I make the card sufficiently large with the intention of creating a display. For example:

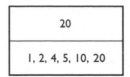

20
1, 2, 4, 5, 10, 20

Clearly the example above is a 'cleaned' up, ordered version showing the divisors of 20; students can be encouraged to calculate the divisors before committing their answers to the pieces of card.

At some point a selection of cards from each group showing all the numbers and their divisors from 1 to 100 can be displayed and this can be used as a resource for a whole-class discussion as well as an *aide-mémoire*.

Once a 'working knowledge' of divisors has begun to emerge there are a range of tasks for students to work on. For example:

o list all the numbers with exactly two divisors (prime numbers);
o list all the numbers with an odd amount of divisors (square numbers);
o max factor – find (say) the five numbers which have the highest amount of divisors (up to 100);
o splitting numbers into their prime factors (leading to preliminary work on indices).

This idea works as follows:

○ Start with a number and write down its divisors.
○ Add these divisors together apart from the number itself.
○ For example, the divisors of 12 are 1, 2, 3, 4, 6 and 12.
○ Add these divisors together, apart from number 12, i.e. $1 + 2 + 3 + 4 + 6 = 16$.
○ 16 now becomes the second number in this divisor 'chain'.
○ Adding the divisors of 16 (apart from 16 itself) we have $1 + 2 + 4 + 8 = 15$.

The chain continues as follows:
$12 \rightarrow 16 \rightarrow 15 \rightarrow 9 \rightarrow 4 \rightarrow 3 \rightarrow 1$.

Other starting numbers can subsequently be added to the diagram, for example:

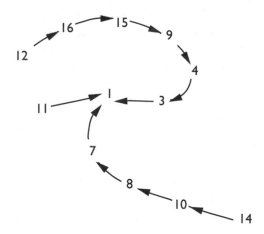

This could make a wall display and be used as a stimulus for discussion, for example:

○ What numbers go directly to 1? Why does this happen?
○ What happens to powers of two, i.e. 2, 4, 8, 16? Why does this happen?

The first idea is more a case of 'divisors in reverse' as it is about working with Lowest Common Multiples (LCMs).

Choose a number, for example, 10.

Partition it into addition pairs, for example, 9 and 1, 8 and 2, 7 and 3, etc.

Determine the LCM of each pair, for example:

○ the LCM of 9 and 1 is 9;
○ the LCM of 8 and 2 is 8;
○ the LCM of 7 and 3 is 21.

The idea is to find the *largest* LCM that appears in a completed list, so that students can try to predict which number pair for any starting value produces the largest LCM.

Students might similarly explore lowest LCMs.

The final idea is another 'practise and consolidation' type of task where the context is to classify numbers as 'Abundant', 'Deficient' or 'Perfect'. These terms are defined according to whether the sum of the divisors (excluding the number itself) is greater than, less than or equal to the number under consideration.

For example, the number 12 is abundant because its divisors of 1, 2, 3, 4 and 6 total to 16 which is greater than 12.

The number 10 is deficient because its divisors of 1, 2 and 5 total to 8 which is less than 10.

Perfect numbers are very rare, once the first four have been found students will need to start searching in the millions to find the next, so most numbers can be classified as 'abundant' or 'deficient'.

There are several problems based upon the idea of the speed at which growth occurs as a result of continually doubling. A classic problem is the grains of rice and the chessboard problem. Here a story about placing one grain of rice on the first square, two grains of rice on the second square, four grains of rice on the third square . . . leads to a question about how many grains of rice there will be if this process continues for all 64 squares.

The important concept is for students to see how quickly the values increase; such problems also cause students to work on the arithmetic of doubling and, as in the problem above, addition. Here are two more problems based upon the same concept.

1   Take a sheet of newspaper and tear it in half.
    Place the two halves together. This is Stage 1.
    Tear Stage 1 pile in half and place these two halves together. This is Stage 2.
    Repeat this process a lot of times.

    The problem is as follows: If the paper was, say, 0.01 cm thick what will the height of the pile be after 10 stages, 20 stages, 50 stages?
    What is the smallest number of stages you will need to get higher than Mt Everest?

2   Starting with 1p, how many times must this be doubled to get to £1 million?

I first met this idea in the Association of Teachers of Mathematics (ATM) journal *Mathematics Teaching* 84; the purpose is for students to consider properties of numbers and explore a different branch of mathematics, i.e. modular, or 'clock' arithmetic.

To illustrate how modular arithmetic works an example of mod 6 is given below.

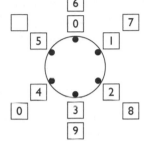

In mod 6 all numbers are represented by one of the following values: 0, 1, 2, 3, 4, 5.

So 6 is represented by zero, 7 is represented by 1, 8 is represented by 2, and so on.

This idea is to consider what happens when numbers are successively doubled in different mods. In mod 6, starting with 1, a doubling chain forms as follows:

$1 \rightarrow 2 \rightarrow 4 \rightarrow 8$. However, 8 in mod 6 is 2, so we gain the following: $1 \rightarrow 2 \leftrightarrow 4$.

Considering chains for numbers that have not so far appeared i.e. 0, 3 and 5, we gain the following in formation: $0 \rightarrow 0 \quad 3 \rightarrow 0 \quad 5 \rightarrow 4 \leftrightarrow 2$.

Collecting all this information together we have: $1 \rightarrow 2 \leftrightarrow 4 \rightarrow 5$ and $3 \rightarrow 0$.

Exploring doubling chains in mod 7, the following three diagrams are formed:

The task is for students, working in groups, to produce a lot of information for doubling in different mods, say up to mod 50, with different mods allocated to different groups. Using sugar paper and large marker pens students can produce a display for analysis.

DOUBLING IN MODULAR ARITHMETIC

EXPLORING UNIT DIGITS

This idea is about students exploring the unit digits for different sequences of numbers. The important issue is for students to learn more about the properties of numbers which exist in different patterns.

For example:

The unit digits for multiples of two are:

2, 4, 6, 8, 0, 2, 4, etc.

The unit digits for multiples of three are:

3, 6, 9, 2, 5, 8, 1, 4, 7, 0, 3, 6, 9, etc.

Upon analysis, the multiples of two contain just five of the digits whereas multiples of three contain all ten digits.

○ What unit digit patterns exist for other sets of multiples?

○ How are the unit digits of multiples of three and multiples of seven connected?

○ What is the pattern of unit digits for the sequence of square numbers?

○ Which numbers do not appear as unit digits for square numbers?

○ Is there a pattern of unit digits for the sequence of cube numbers?

○ Start with 1 and keep doubling: 2, 4, 8, 16, 32, 64, 128 . . . . What, therefore, is the pattern in the unit digits, (excluding the first term of 1), for powers of 2? What happens if we start with 3 and keep doubling?

○ Start with 1 and start trebling (i.e. 1, 3, 27, 81, 243 . . . the powers of 3). What is the pattern of the units digits now?

○ What happens if we start with 2 and keep trebling?

○ Is there any pattern of unit digits in the Fibonacci sequence? You will need to be quite persistent to be sure you have answered this question.

○ What groups or sequences of numbers are there which do not appear to have any pattern in the unit digits?

One of the complexities of teaching, particularly in a secondary school, is that of waiting for a class to arrive. This can take several minutes, particularly if the class arrives from different subject areas. The following idea is typical of the kind of puzzling out type of task I have used with classes in order to bridge the time between the first and the last student arriving.

This and similar tasks are ones I offer only as a way of getting a class engaged with something as soon as they enter the room and which I can describe by displaying a few instructions on the board/screen, for example:

1 Throw five dice (e.g. 3, 3, 5, 1, 6).
2 Try to make a total of 100 using the following rules:
   o you have to use every number once only in any order;
   o each number must be used as a single digit;
   o you can use any combination of $+$, $-$, $\times$, $\div$ and brackets.

For the numbers 3, 3, 5, 1, and 6 a possible solution is: $(6 \times 3 + 3 - 1) \times 5$.

With a pack of cards I take out all the court cards and the tens then turn over five of the remaining 36 cards; again the problem is to combine these using the rules to make 100.

This idea is one I have used several times and first came across in *Points of Departure 2*, one of many excellent ATM publications. The idea is an adaptation from *POD2* and requires square-dot grid paper and works as follows.

Consider the following 'sequences':

o Start 2, 1, 2, 2, 1, 2 Finish
o Start 3, 1, 3, 2, 2, 3, 1, 3 Finish
o Start 4, 1, 4, 2, 3, 3, 2, 4, 1, 4 Finish
o Start 5, 1, 5, 2, 4, 3, 3, 4, 2, 5, 1, 5 Finish

What will the next few sequences be?

Now draw each sequence on a square-dot grid as follows:

o Choose a start point and draw the first length as a horizontal line from right to left.
o Next turn 'right' through an internal angle of 90° (or an external angle of 270°) and draw the next length.
o Keep turning right and draw each line until you reach the 'Finish'.

Once you have drawn each of the four sequences above try drawing each one of them as fast as you can. Now try drawing the next few diagrams at speed. The idea here is to produce a rhythm to enable the artist to 'feel' how the pattern works.

For each diagram the following questions can be explored with the possibility of students trying to produce general results:

o How many instructions are there are for each sequence?
o What is the total length of each sequence?
o What is the enclosed area for each sequence?
o How many 4-node points are there on each diagram?
o How many 3-node points are there on each diagram?
o How many 3- and 4-node points are there on each diagram?

This is a simple-to-pose problem holding hidden complexities and is, therefore, useful for offering to students of different ages and attainments.

Choose a two-digit number and write it down, for example   39

Reverse it	93
Add	132 (stage 1)
Reverse it	231
Add	363 (stage 2)

Stop here because the answer, 363, is palindromic

The number 39 can now be classified as a 2-stage number.

How many stages do other numbers take?

Challenges such as finding 4-stage and 6-stage numbers will provide a class with plenty to work on.

If different stages are colour coded, students might make use of a 100 square and colour in every number according to how many stages each takes. There will, of course, be several zero-stage numbers that are already palindromic such as 11, 22, 33, etc. Students might be encouraged to explore why palindromic answers produced in this way are all multiples of 11. Trying to explain why this is the case will provide students with an interesting challenge.

A harder problem is to consider palindromic multiplication when two two-digit numbers are used, for example: $96 \times 23 = 32 \times 69$.

The smallest palindromic product of two two-digit numbers that some PGCE students found was 504, proving me wrong when I had thought 806 was the smallest product!

o What is the palindromic multiplication to make 504?
o Is there a smaller palindromic product?
o What palindromic multiplication gives 806?

Asking students to generate more examples, explore the underlying structure of the process and, ultimately, to try to prove the result will provide worthy challenges.

19

This is another idea from the ATM *Points of Departure* publications.

Choose a number and ask each student to individually write four or five partitions. For example, using the number ten one student might write:

5 + 5
2 + 3 + 5
4 + 5 + 1
6 + 4
1 + 1 + 1 + 1 + 1 + 1 + 1 + 1 + 1 + 1

Turning each addition sign into a multiplication sign the following products are gained:

$5 \times 5 = 25$
$2 \times 3 \times 5 = 30$
$4 \times 5 \times 1 = 20$
$6 \times 4 = 24$
$1 \times 1 \times 1 \times 1 \times 1 \times 1 \times 1 \times 1 \times 1 \times 1 = 1$

At this point each student could be asked to provide one of their answers and these could be written on the board/screen. The intention here is for students to see the different range of answers that are possible. A further task at this point can be for students to try to produce the partitions that led to the answers provided.

The main point of this task is for students to explore which partition produces the maximum product. A write-up of one student's work on this problem appears in the ATM journal *Mathematics Teaching* 127, pp 26–27.

An extension for this task is to consider what happens if the rule of partitioning into decimal values is allowed. What will the maximum product be under this circumstance?

Take half a dozen pictures from a magazine and copy/photo reduce them onto a sheet of A4 paper. The pictures could be of anything, a shoe, a car, a camera, a person ... anything at all.

This idea is for students to try to work out what approximate scale factors must be applied to each item to enlarge them to life size, so the person can wear the shoe, sit in the car, use the camera, etc.

One way of developing the task could be for students to work in a small group to agree upon the scale factors of enlargement they would use and then for one group to compare their answers with those from another group. This will have the potential for students to discuss degrees of accuracy of the calculations they have done.

SCALE FACTORS

This idea is about giving students an answer and asking them to find questions or ways of producing the answer. Students might write stories where a certain number appears with some prominence so that the stories give meaning to the number. The aims are for students:

○ to find different ways of arriving at a given numbers;
○ to help them recognize different properties numbers have;
○ to see numbers arise in different contexts.

One might decide to choose a number for the week, where students are asked to work out (and display) their ideas. This could make a useful homework task, particularly if parents/guardians are encouraged to take part.

The following statements are all about the number 45; they could of course all be turned into questions.

○ 45 is the angle between North and North East, North East and East, etc.
○ 45 is the sum of two squares $(x^2 + y^2)$, (therefore, x, y, $\sqrt{45}$ is a right-angled triangle).
○ 45 is the difference of two squares and, therefore, the product of $(a + b)(a - b)$.
○ 45 is the speed 'single' records rotate in one minute.
○ 45 is the ninth triangular number $(1 + 2 + 3 + \ldots 8 + 9)$.
○ In a right-angled isosceles triangle there are two 45° angles.
○ Tan 45° = 1.
○ The prime factors of 45 are $3^2 \times 5$.
○ 45 is palindromic when written in binary (or base 2), i.e. 1 0 1 1 0 1.
○ The best 45 minutes I spent at a football match was seeing Liverpool score three second-half goals against Olympiakos.

What stories can you make up about the number 45?

This idea can be used to help students consolidate their knowledge of properties of numbers by posing questions based upon the outcome of throwing three dice. It works as follows.

Throw three dice and use +, −, ×, ÷ and brackets to combine the numbers showing on the top face of the dice to gain different values, for example.

○ the highest total;
○ the lowest total;
○ the highest prime number;
○ the lowest prime number;
○ the highest square number;
○ the lowest square number.

Other target values could be to gain the highest and lowest:

○ triangle numbers;
○ Fibonacci sequence numbers;
○ Lucas sequence numbers (i.e. 1, 3, 4, 7, 11 . . .);
○ numbers nearest to zero;
○ negative numbers.

This idea is similar to the 'classic' problem about finding five numbers (or weights) and the operation of addition only to produce all the possible values from 1 to 31. This is an interesting task to work on, not least of all because the solution set is 16, 8, 4, 2, and 1 which are the binary (base 2) column headings.

The 'Take three numbers' idea is similar to this problem but allows the use of subtraction as well as addition. The problem is to find the 'best' three numbers that can be used to make all the possible values from 1 to a value somewhere in between 10 and 20. I have not revealed what this highest value is in order to offer the reader a challenge and engage in the pleasure of puzzling.

For example, if the three numbers were 3, 4 and 6 then I can make the following:

$1 = 4 - 3$

$2 = 6 - 4$

$3 = 3$

$4 = 4$

$5 = 6 + 3 - 4$

$6 = 6$

$7 = 3 + 4$

Eight cannot be made, so with 3, 4 and 6 the highest value, including all the possible values from 1 upwards, is 7.

With four numbers all the values from 1 to 40 can be made and once students have solved the earlier problem this one will be easy!

This problem can provide an opportunity for students to find negative as well as positive solutions.

There are many mathematical tasks that can be created using strips of paper; the following idea was suggested to me by Anna McCafferty a PGCE student.

o Fold a strip of paper into a number of equal portions (say a minimum of four and a maximum of eight).
o On top of the first portion write a number between one and ten.
o On the second portion write a function, for example: +2.
o On the third portion write another function, for example: ×4, and so on.

The idea is for students to carry out some mental arithmetic to try to work out the final answer as each of the functions are applied to the previous value.

For example, the start number could be 3 and the functions +2, ×4, −8, ÷2 and +5.

Students can work in pairs, each making a strip, choosing the number of portions and the start number and calculating the answer. Partners then have to work out what each others' answers are once all the functions have been applied.

Expressing the above as a sequence of functions using a start number (s):

s	$s + 2$	$4s + 8$	$2s$	$2s + 5$

will provide an opportunity for students to write expressions using brackets, for example,
$[(s+2)\times4-8]\div2+5$.

The task could also be turned around and used as a context for solving equations. For example, if the start number s is unknown and the answer a is given, the idea is for a partner to work out the value of s.

For example, what is the value of s if $[(s + 2) \times 4 − 8] \div 2 + 5 = 11$?

IDEA
22

DOMINO DELIGHT

Using a set of dominoes as a resource for the mathematics classroom can provide students with opportunities to engage with some interesting ideas. Just exploring the structure that exists in a set of dominoes, in terms of how many there are up to 6–6, how many up to 5–5, 4–4, etc., is one way of generating the triangular number sequence.

PROBLEM 1
Find a way of adding together all the spots on all the dominoes using a set up to 6–6 without needing to count each spot!

PROBLEM 2
How many spots will there be for smaller and larger sets of dominoes?

The next four problems are based upon a double six set with all the doubles removed, thus leaving 15 dominoes.

Consider all these 15 dominoes as 'proper' fractions (i.e. where the numerator is smaller than the denominator).

PROBLEM 3 (A)
What do all these dominoes, as proper fractions, sum to?

PROBLEM 3 (B)
Split the dominoes into three sets of five so the total for each set is the same.

PROBLEM 4 (A)
What is the sum of the 15 dominoes if they are treated as improper (or vulgar) fractions?

PROBLEM 4 (B)
Split the dominoes into three sets of five so the total for each set is the same.

For this idea I offer an alternative way of displaying fraction walls made from a series of strips of paper placed horizontally underneath one another. Often the fractional amounts are written in the middle of each fractional piece, for example:

½		½	
$\frac{1}{3}$	$\frac{1}{3}$		$\frac{1}{3}$
$\frac{1}{4}$	$\frac{1}{4}$	$\frac{1}{4}$	$\frac{1}{4}$

An alternative way of displaying fraction walls is to write each strip as a number line.

The top strip will have 0, ½, ²⁄₂ written at the beginning, the middle and the end.

The next line down will have 0, ⅓, ⅔ and ³⁄₃ written on it.

The next line down will have 0, ¼ , ²⁄₄, ¾ and ⁴⁄₄ written on it.

By taking the strips of paper down to say twelfths, students can look for equivalent sets of fractions and also compare fractional sizes, for example, which is the biggest: ⅔ or ⁵⁄₇?

A development of this is to make two strips for each fractional division and place one strip underneath the other. Writing fractional divisions on one strip and decimal equivalents on the other. For example:

| 0 | ⅕ | ⅖ | ⅗ | ⅘ | ⁵⁄₅ |
| 0 | 0.2 | 0.4 | 0.6 | 0.8 | 1.0 |

Comparisons between fractions and decimals can be seen.

A further development is to make a 'Toblerone' shape (or triangular-based prisms) to produce three rectangular faces. These can be used to write and compare fractions, decimals and percentages.

FRACTION WALLS AS NUMBER LINES

This problem is about a confused, love-struck frog who cannot make up her mind but happens to be expert at measuring fractional distances. The situation is as follows:

Felicity Frog is sitting on a stone right in the middle of a river. On one bank are all her mates who have been out on a tadpole night prior to Felicity's marriage to Herbert. On the other bank sits Herbert awaiting his true love to join him. The problem is that Felicity just cannot decide whether to swim to her pals, who are shouting to her: 'You'll be tied to the kitchen sink . . . ' and 'Don't do it . . . ', or to the other bank where Herbert is dolefully croaking his love-song to her.

Felicity sets off and swims towards Herbert, but when she is exactly halfway between the middle of the river and Herbert she has a change of mind and swims back towards her pals. After swimming exactly half the distance she originally swam towards Herbert, Felicity has another change of mind, at which point she swims half the previous distance back towards Herbert. Assuming Felicity continue in this state of indecision, where will she end up?

The problem can be developed by changing the fractional distance, say to ⅓, ⅔, ¾ or any non-vulgar fraction . . . where does that description come from? The idea is to see for each fractional distance where the final point in the river is and how this compares to the fraction under exploration.

Who said mathematics isn't sexy?

The ideas below are intended to help students use and apply their knowledge of fractions and, as such, they will need to have some knowledge of subtracting and adding fractions.

PROBLEM 1

Differencing and differencing

Write a list of fractions which have denominators in the sequence 2, 3, 4, 5, 6, 7 . . . i.e. $\frac{1}{2}$, $\frac{1}{3}$, $\frac{1}{4}$, $\frac{1}{5}$, $\frac{1}{6}$, $\frac{1}{7}$, etc.

Find the differences between adjacent pairs of fractions.

Adjacent fraction		*Difference*
$\frac{1}{2} - \frac{1}{3}$	=	$\frac{1}{6}$
$\frac{1}{3} - \frac{1}{4}$	=	$\frac{1}{12}$
$\frac{1}{4} - \frac{1}{5}$	=	. . .

What do you notice about these answers? What happens if you now take the difference of the differences?

PROBLEM 2

Cumulative calculations

Write a list of fractions which have denominators of powers of 2, i.e. 1, 2, 4, 8, 16 . . .

$\frac{1}{1}$, $\frac{1}{2}$, $\frac{1}{4}$, $\frac{1}{8}$, $\frac{1}{16}$, etc.

What happens when the following calculations are made?

$\frac{1}{1}$

$\frac{1}{1} + \frac{1}{2}$

$\frac{1}{1} + \frac{1}{2} + \frac{1}{4}$

Write a list of fractions which have denominators in the triangular number sequence, i.e.

$\frac{1}{1}$, $\frac{1}{3}$, $\frac{1}{6}$, $\frac{1}{10}$, $\frac{1}{15}$, etc.

What happens when the following calculations are made?

$\frac{1}{1}$	=	$\frac{1}{1}$
$\frac{1}{1} + \frac{1}{3}$	=	$\frac{4}{3}$
$\frac{1}{1} + \frac{1}{3} + \frac{1}{6}$	=	$\frac{9}{6}$
$\frac{1}{1} + \frac{1}{3} + \frac{1}{6} + \frac{1}{10}$	=	. . .

Explore the pattern in the answers.

What happens if the sequence starts:

$\frac{1}{3}$

$\frac{1}{3} + \frac{1}{6}$

$\frac{1}{3} + \frac{1}{6} + \frac{1}{10}$.

Trying to find ways of engaging students with problems involving percentages, which go beyond the standard exercise type of format where short questions are typically presented as: find 20 per cent of £42, is not always easy. The following two problems are intended to deepen students' understanding of how percentages work.

PROBLEM 1

Choose an amount of money and increase it by 10 per cent.

Take this new total and decrease it by 10 per cent.

We now have slightly less money than we had to start off with.

What happens if we increase an amount by 20 per cent then decrease the total by 20 per cent?

What happens if we increase by x per cent then decrease by x per cent?

PROBLEM 2

Choose an amount of money (e.g. €100).

Increase this by 10 per cent (€110).

Increase the new amount by 10 per cent (€121).

Keep increasing each previous amount by 10% until you at least double your money.

How many increases does it take to at least double your money?

Repeat the above but start with a different amount of money. How many increases does it take to double your money now?

How many increases does it take to double your money if the constant increase is 20 per cent or 5 per cent?

How many increases would it take to at least triple your money, for increases of 10 per cent, 20 per cent or 5 per cent?

If an increase is a constant measure of time, then how long would it take to exactly double your money for 10 per cent increases?

There are opportunities here for graphing results and constructing a formula for Compound Interest.

Puzzles to NAG (Number, Algebra and Graphs) your students with

The Fibonacci sequence appears in a variety of natural contexts and has many intriguing properties. There are also many ways the sequence can be generated. For example:

○ The number of ways to ascend a set of stairs by going up one or two stairs at each step.
○ The number of ways of making different amounts of money using £1 and £2 coins.
○ The number of ways of filling a 2-by-n 'path' using paving slabs measuring 2-by-1 and 1-by-2. For example in a 2-by-4 path, there are five possible solutions.
○ On a spreadsheet by typing:
  1 in cell A1,
  1 in cell A2,
  = A1 + A2 in cell A3 then filling down.

The following ideas are based upon tasks once the sequence has been generated

EXTENDING THE SEQUENCE.
Having generated the first few values of the sequence, work out all the values up to, say, the twentieth term. This can be a useful context for practising mental arithmetic.

How many terms does it take to get above 1 million?

GENERATING THE GOLDEN RATIO (1.618034 . . .)
This is gained by dividing successive terms, i.e.
$2 \div 1, 3 \div 2, 5 \div 3 \ldots 10946 \div 6765$.

By reversing these calculations, i.e.
$1 \div 2, 2 \div 3, 3 \div 5 \ldots 6765 \div 10946$, a result of the previous limit less 1 is gained.

This task might be used as a context for setting up a quadratic equation, i.e. $1/\Phi = \Phi - 1$ leading to $\Phi^2 - \Phi = 1$.

GRAPHING THE ABOVE RESULTS
By graphing the two sets of results from the previous task on the same axes, students will have an opportunity to appreciate the notion of the values settling out to the Golden Ratio (Φ) and to the Golden Ratio minus 1 ($\Phi - 1$).

These are further ideas that students can explore based upon the Fibonacci sequence and they draw upon a range of mathematical concepts and skills, for example, working with negative numbers, using and applying algebra and forming generalizations.

SUMMING A FIBONACCI SEQUENCE UP TO THE TENTH TERM

This sum can be calculated by multiplying the seventh term by 11. The question is, why? For example: 7, 4, 11, 15, 26, 41, 67, 108, 175, 283 sums to 737 which is 67×11.

SOLVING 'NUMBER CELL' PROBLEMS.

This idea is aimed at developing students' symbolic manipulating skills. Students can work in pairs, each producing a number of five-cell sequences, for example: 7, 3, 10, 13, 23 or 5, −2, 3, 1, 4, and so on.

Having done this they give their partner the first and the last value for each set of numbers, for example: 7 _ _ _ 23 or 5 _ _ _ 4. Students then have to try to calculate each other's missing values.

A development is for students to construct a formula to describe how f (the first number) and l (the last number) in each five-cell can be manipulated to find m (the middle number).

Using the symbols f, l and m, the equation $m = \frac{1}{3}(f + l)$ can be constructed.

Students can check this works for any values.

A further exploration aimed at producing formulae for finding the middle values when seven, nine and eleven-cell, etc. are considered (given the first and last values), reveals an interesting result. This will challenge students to construct formulae based upon the information gathered.

This idea begins with writing the numbers 1, 2, 3, 4 and 5 in any order in a (pentagonal) ring.

Next, calculate the positive difference between adjacent pairs of numbers and write these answers in between (perhaps in another colour to differentiate them from the five starting numbers).

Now add together all the differences and write the total in the middle of the ring.

In the example below the result can be written as follows:

$(3 - 1) + (4 - 1) + (5 - 4) + (5 - 2) + (3 - 2)$ which is equal to 10.

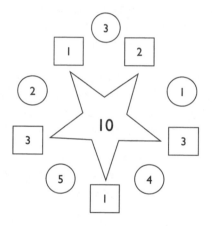

Questions can now be worked on such as:

○ What other totals can be achieved using the same five starting numbers written in a different order?

○ Why can only a certain set of totals be made?

○ What happens if we start with 6, 7, 8, etc. consecutive numbers? How many different answers are there for each situation?

○ Generalize the minimum total for n consecutive numbers starting at 1?

○ Generalize the maximum total for n consecutive numbers starting at 1?

The following ideas are developments from Idea 29.

1   What happens if, instead of finding the positive difference, we calculate the product between adjacent pairs and total up these products? What answers are possible now?

2   What happens if we calculate quotients and total these results? Because division is not commutative we will need to determine a direction of travel around the ring of numbers. However, this can generate two further problems:

    ○ What is the total if the direction of travel around the ring is reversed?

    ○ What is the total if the values created from adjacent pairs are always written as fractions?

3   What happens if we turn adjacent pairs of numbers into coordinate pairs and these are plotted as points? Students can explore shapes that are produced. Again we will need to be consistent in determining the direction of travel around the ring, although by plotting points using both directions of travel around the ring, the property of reflection in the line $y = x$ can emerge.

    ○ What are the names, symmetries, areas and perimeters of the shapes so formed?

I first met this problem in the 1970s in the seminal text *Starting Points* by Banwell, Saunders and Tahta. The idea is to see how many 'different' arrangements of a given number of dots are possible and how many joins exist for these arrangements. It connects ideas of geometric arrangements, with simple counting and some algebraic generalization, as such it would be suitable for students from a wide attainment range.

To see how many 'different' arrangements of a given number of dots can be made, I would ask students to draw a selection of arrangements for five dots on the board/screen. Having collected some examples, students can analyse them in terms of how many straight line joins are created.

The following more detailed description is one I offer to the reader, though not one I would give to students. This is because I want students to engage with some ambiguity to cause them to make their own decisions about how to arrange the dots and how many joins are possible.

For example, with five dots in a straight line we create four joins.

However, if the dots are arranged as in the diagram below, we gain seven joins.

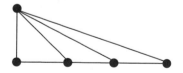

These joins must be straight lines though clearly not of the same length. If all five dots are arranged in the shape of a pentagon, we can form ten joins, which is the maximum.

The problem is to find what other different arrangements/ number of joins are possible. This can lead to students classifying the types of structures created, searching for number patterns and, where appropriate, trying to generalize sets of results formed for different numbers of dots and types of arrangements.

IDEA

32

SPROUTS

Euro-sceptics may be relieved to know this idea has nothing to do with Brussels.

Sprouts is a game for two people requiring cooperation and provides opportunities for strategic thinking, problem-solving, careful counting, some pattern spotting, looking for a 'closed' generalization and a bit of fun.

The game is based upon a situation involving nodes, arcs and regions where:

○ A node is a small blob (or a big dot).
○ A region is an area bounded by at least two arcs.
○ An arc is a line (curved or straight) joining two nodes.

The game is played as follows:

○ Draw two, three or four nodes on a piece of paper.
○ Players take turns to join pairs of nodes with arcs.
○ As soon as an arc is drawn a new node is drawn on it (i.e. a new node 'sprouts' on the arc).

The game continues using the following rules:

1 Every time a pair of nodes is joined by an arc, a new node sprouts on the arc just drawn (this new node effectively splits the arc into two shorter arcs).
2 When a node has three arcs coming out from it the node becomes defunct, deceased, dead. It is crossed out and cannot be used again.
3 Players are not allowed to draw an arc to join two nodes by crossing over an existing arc.
4 The same pair of nodes can be joined by more than one arc.

The winner is the person who draws the final arc. Once a game is completed, count the nodes, regions and arcs for the resulting diagram. We also need to count an extra region around the outside (imaging drawing a frame around the diagram and this produces a further region).

Students can play several games and gather the required data to look for the connection between nodes, regions and arcs.

The following idea is one I have used with Year 10 students in mixed-attainment groups. Because the problem can be both simplified and developed to varying degrees, all students can gain different levels of achievement.

The problem involves students drawing shapes from a given number of squares (n) joined by full edge to full edge. Information is then extracted from each diagram drawn; how many places four squares meet at different points (m), together with the perimeter of the shape (p).

For example, if the squares are joined as follows there are three places where four squares meet:

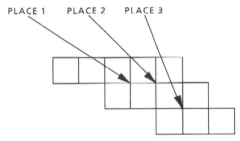

PLACE 1   PLACE 2   PLACE 3

so $m = 3$ and $p = 20$.

If the squares are joined, say, in the shape of a 3-by-4 rectangle then $m = 6$ and $p = 14$. The idea is to form connections between n, m and p.

I have introduced the problem by inviting students to use 12 squares and gather a range of different sets of results. With this information students can explore patterns and connections between n, m and p.

Using smaller numbers of squares may help to simplify the problem, however, as explorers of mathematics, this is a decision students need to make for themselves.

Using equilateral triangles and regular hexagons can provide extensions to the problem.

TURNING INSIDE-OUT

This problem is one I would describe as a 'closed' problem yet is another active task that has potential for fun and laughter, particularly if the performers do not solve the problem too speedily. This might sound to run contrary to what students are mainly intended to do in classrooms – correctly solve problems. However, if engaging with a spot of stuckness can occur simultaneously with enjoyment and all in the name of learning mathematics, this will do for me.

Ask five or six students to stand holding hands in a ring facing inwards. The challenge is for students to turn themselves inside-out, without letting go of any hands, so they remain in a ring and face outwards (without having their hands crossed-over).

My funniest moment with this idea was working with a Year 8 group when they got themselves into a real tangle.

As students solve this problem, which is not actually that difficult to work out, they can try to solve it for different numbers of people in the ring.

Once a solution is realized the following questions can be posed:

○ Can students find a way of describing the process using symbols and diagrams?
○ Can students generalize the situation for *n* people in a ring?

Ask volunteers to come to the board/screen and write pairs of positive whole numbers that add up together to make 10.

Once a collection of answers has been generated students can a) write the results in an ordered way, or b) turn the pairs of values into coordinate pairs and plot them on a graph.

Once this graph has been drawn further questions might be:

o What if one of the values is $4\frac{1}{2}$? Does 'this' point, i.e. $(4\frac{1}{2}, 5\frac{1}{2})$, also live on the graph?
o What if one of the values is 3.8? Where does this point lie on the graph?
o How many different answers are possible now?
o What happens if one of the two numbers is 13? Now what happens to the graph?
o What if the problem is to find two numbers that add up to 11? What happens with this graph? How do the two graphs compare?
o How can the graphs be described algebraically?
o Suppose the problem was: One number subtract another number is equal to 5. What does the graph of this situation look like?
o What about: One number subtract another number is equal to negative 5? What does this graph look like?

The ideas here focus on developing students' algebraic thinking and require the 'extended' 100 square to be projected onto a screen/board. The first idea is based upon the concept that any linear sequence can be determined by knowing the base set of multiples upon which the sequence is formed.

On an OHT/PowerPoint image, and using the extended 100 square, circle the first few multiples of two, i.e. 2, 4, 6, 8, 10, then consider the following procedure:

o Establish that these values can be described as $2x$ or $2n$ numbers.

o Now shift the OHT one place to the **L**eft so the numbers 1, 3, 5, 7, 9 become circled.

o Having previously established a shift of one place to the **L**eft is the same as -1, then this new sequence of numbers can be described, algebraically, as $2n - 1$.

Returning each time to the circled numbers 2, 4, 6, 8, 10, different shifts can now be made, e.g. 2 places to the **L**eft creates the sequence $2n - 2$. Three places to the **R**ight creates $2n + 3$. One place **U**p creates $2n + 10$.

Supplying each student with a 100 square and some tracing paper (to serve the same purpose as an OHT), they can create sequences themselves based upon other sets of multiples followed by shifts on the grid.

Each time a new sequence is created and its algebraic description is determined, these can be displayed, particularly if students have access to felt pens and strips of sugar paper. In no time at all dozens of linear sequences and their algebraic descriptions can emerge and be used as a resource for future lessons.

This problem involves adding together any amount of two different numbers and exploring the highest total value that *cannot* be made.

For example, if the two numbers are 3 and 11 these are the values I can and cannot make:

1 – cannot be made
2 – cannot be made
3 = 3
4 – cannot be made
5 – cannot be made
6 = 3 + 3
7 – cannot be made
8 – cannot be made
9 = 3 + 3 + 3
10 – cannot be made
11 = 11
12 = 3 + 3 + 3 + 3
13 – cannot be made
14 = 3 + 11
15 = 3 + 3 + 3 + 3 + 3
16 – cannot be made
17 = 3 + 3 + 11
18 = 3 + 3 + 3 + 3 + 3 + 3
19 – cannot be made
20 = 3 + 3 + 3 + 11
21 = 3 + 3 + 3 + 3 + 3 + 3 + 3
22 = 11 + 11

It is now possible to make every other value because:

23 = 20 (which can be made) + 3
24 = 21 (which can be made) + 3
25 = 22 (which can be made) + 3, etc.

The highest value I cannot make, therefore, using lots of 3s and 11s is 19.

What is the highest value I cannot make for other pairs of numbers?

Students might be encouraged to draw a two-way table.

Can a generalization be formed for (lots of) a and b?

IDEA

38

DIAGONAL DIVERSIONS 1

The following problems are based upon lengths of lines and areas of shapes within regular polygons. The problems are written for students who have acquired knowledge of Pythagoras and trigonometry.

o In a regular pentagon all diagonals are the same length. What is the ratio of the length of a diagonal to the length of a side in a regular pentagon? Students can draw different sized pentagons and compare answers. The result is, of course, going to be 1.618 (to 3 decimal places), i.e. the Golden Ratio. If the inverse ratio is taken, between the length of a side and the length of a diagonal, then the answer will be 0.618, or 1.618 − 1. As with Idea 27, this task might also be used to create the quadratic $\Phi^2 − \Phi − 1 = 0$ arising from $\frac{1}{\Phi} = \Phi − 1$.

o Again for a regular pentagon, when a single diagonal is cut off, an isosceles triangle and an isosceles trapezium are formed. What is the ratio of the areas of these shapes?

o How many different length diagonals are there in different regular polygons?

o What different ratios of lengths of pairs of diagonals exist?

o What different ratios exist when comparing the lengths of different diagonals to the length of the side of the polygon?

My thanks goes to Peter Hampson, the headteacher at my last school who showed me this trick which I have used many times in lots of lessons.

1 Using a full pack of cards turn over the top card and call out its face value (Jack, Queen and King cards count as face value of 10).
2 Count out extra cards so the face value of the first card and extra cards add up to a total of 12. For example, if the first card is a 9, count three more cards to make 12 and place these underneath the 9. This now makes the first pile (p).
3 Turn over the next card from the remaining pack and repeat as before. If this card is a 5 then count out a further seven cards (to make up to 12), place these under the 5, and make a second pile.
4 Keep repeating this until you reach a situation where there are not enough cards in the remaining pack to make a total of 12. Place these cards in a separate remainder pile (r).

Without looking at the cards on the top of each pile, it is possible to work out the total sum of the cards by knowing how many piles and how many remainder cards there are.

The following is a natural development and provides in-context opportunities for students to construct formulae to show how the total (T) can be calculated by knowing the number of piles (p) and the number of remaining cards (r).

Trying to explain *why* the formula connecting p, r and T works will provide a further, worthy challenge.

A development of this task is to change the variables within the problem. Suppose a pack of cards consisted of four suits with only ten cards per suit, or five suits and ten cards in each, what would the 'magic' totals be in each case?

How would the formula connecting p and r with T change?

LONGEST PATH THROUGH A RECTANGLE

This idea is one I have used to develop students' understanding of quadratic sequences and requires students to have access to 1 cm-square grid paper and works as follows:

○ Draw a rectangle on square grid paper, for example 7 by 4.
○ Choose a grid point on one edge of the rectangle but not at a corner.
○ Draw horizontal and vertical lines, which do not meet or cross each other to create a path to the opposite side (again not a corner).

The task is to find the longest possible path.
Using a 7-by-4 rectangle the longest path is 19 as in the diagram below:

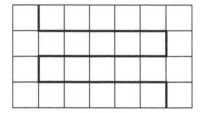

Students can attempt to generalize for rectangles measuring 7 by n.
What happens with 6-by-n rectangles?
What is the general result for any rectangle m by n?
What happens if the problem is based upon an equilateral triangle drawn on an isometric-dot grid? For this problem the idea is to move from a point on one side (similarly not at a corner) to either of the other two sides and again taking the longest route possible. Perhaps, unsurprisingly, the result is connected to, though not the same as, the triangular number sequence.

The phrase 'Students being responsible for their learning' is one that springs to my mind when I use an idea such as 'Number route problems'. Here students set up and solve each other's problems and I am interested in how to create a culture of problem-posing and problem-solving so students are encouraged to engage with such ways of working. One aspect of the teacher's role is to model a situation so students know what they need to do to develop skills and concepts.

This idea is to set up situations such as:

○ I start with a number (s), multiply it by six to gain an answer (a).

○ I start with the same number (s), add 24 and multiply this total by two to gain the same answer (a).

○ Using these statements, what was my starting number?

Clearly guesswork and trial and improvement will eventually provide the correct values for s and a and, in the first instance, this is fine. However, this task also has rich potential for students to practise and consolidate solving equations with an unknown on both sides of the equation.

Thus, in the example above we have the following:

$6s = a$

$(s + 24) \times 2 = a$.

Which can be combined to form the equality:

$6s = 2s + 48$. Solving this we have $s = 12$ and $a = 72$.

By choosing their own starting values and answers, students can easily create such number route problems.

The idea can be developed as follows:

○ Start with a number (s), square it and add five to get an answer (a).

○ Start with the same number, multiply it by seven and subtract one to get the same answer. Because the situation creates a quadratic equation, there will be two solutions, i.e. $s = 6$ and $s = 1$.

Algebraically the equation $s^2 + 5 = 7s - 1$ can be constructed leading to $s^2 - 7s + 6 = 0$. Factorizing this we gain $(s - 6)(s - 1) = 0$.

3 'MULTIPLIED' BY 2 IS 8

This problem is an exploration of the traditional multiplication system on a square grid turned through 45° and works as follows.

On the 'turned' grid, draw a three-dot by two-dot rectangle.

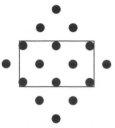

Counting the number of dots in the whole rectangle we have a total of eight. In this system therefore, 3 * 2 = 8.

(I deliberately decide not use the multiplication sign and seek to ensure that students don't confuse this 'different' system with the usual multiplication system.)

o   What is 5 * 3?
o   What is 7 * 2?

This can be developed to produce a two-way combination table under the * system.

Questions that arise can be:

o   What are the 'square' numbers in this system?
o   What is the general term for a 'square' number *n* * *n*?
o   What is the general term for a 'rectangular' number *m* * *n*?
o   What are the 'prime' numbers in this system?

The above system is one based upon dots on the perimeter dots being √2 apart. If the grid is turned through a different angle, so dots on the perimeter of a shape are √5 apart. Another different set of results are created and exploring this and other 'turned' systems will provide many opportunities for pattern spotting and algebraic generalization.

Puzzles to cause your students to *shape up*

If I could take just one resource with me to Mars to demonstrate how I teach mathematics to its inhabitants it would certainly be a square 9-pin geoboard.

There are many problems that can be posed using the equipment and some are:

1 Find all the possible non-congruent triangles.
   - Describe their properties and align these to their names.
   - Classify them in terms of equal lengths of sides and right-angles.
   - Prove a complete set has been made.
   - Find how many congruent triangles there are for each different one. This can provide an opportunity for students to engage in the vocabulary of rotation, reflection and translation.
   - Calculate the area of each triangle (assuming the area of one square is 1 unit).
   - Measure the perimeter of each triangle (to the nearest mm).
   - Students who have met Pythagoras' theorem and surds can work out the different possible lengths on a 9-pin board, i.e. 1, 2, $\sqrt{2}$, $2\sqrt{2}$ and $\sqrt{5}$. Students can then use these to determine the perimeter of each triangle.
   - Code the possible lengths as a, (for length 1), b (for length $\sqrt{2}$) and c (for length $\sqrt{5}$) then write the perimeter of each triangle in terms of a, b and c. This will provide students with an elementary experience of collecting like terms.
2 Find all the possible quadrilaterals.
3 Find all the possible pentagons.

For problems 2 and 3, all the ideas in the first problem can be applied to the shapes created.

Further problems on a square 9-pin geoboard:

1 How many different vectors are there? This can be developed to consider how many vectors there are on 16-dot and 25-dot grids and a general result can be looked for.

   o How many pairs of parallel vectors can be made on different sizes of geoboards?

   o How many pairs of vectors can be made that are perpendicular to one another?

2 By marking out the geoboard as a coordinate grid, a problem can be posed about how many different straight lines there are and describing them in terms of $y = mx + c$. Again this problem can be developed by increasing the size of the geoboard.

   o Draw a pair of lines that intersect but not at one of the marked grid points. What are the coordinates of the point of intersection? How many non-grid point intersections can be found? What are the coordinates of each one?

3 Is it possible to draw an equilateral triangle on a square-based geoboard? For example, on a 9-pin geoboard, the nearest we can get to an equilateral triangle is an isosceles triangle with lengths 2, $\sqrt{5}$ and $\sqrt{5}$. Can an equilateral triangle be drawn on a 16-pin, a 25-pin . . . a n-by-n board?

4 Make two shapes on the same 9-pin board so they cross over each other. What is the area of the shape formed by the overlap of the original two shapes?

UNFOLDING AND LINE SYMMETRY

This is another simple idea to set up yet provides students with plenty to think about and work, on the question: 'Can you show you have found all the possible solutions?'

Draw some polygons, for example a right-angled isosceles triangle, a parallelogram, an asymmetrical trapezium containing two right angles, etc. Each of these shapes are the outcomes after other 'initial' shapes have been folded once in half. The idea is for students to visualize and draw all the possible initial shapes that led to the final shapes.

For example, if the final shape is an asymmetrical trapezium with two right angles there are four initial shapes that can be unfolded to produce this shape.

These are:

o an L-shaped hexagon with one concave angle;
o two pentagons, one having a concave angle;
o an isosceles trapezium.

Such a collection of shapes will provide students with a context to engage in the vocabulary of shapes, such as properties and names.

Furthermore, if the angles of the original shape are known, the angles in each final shape can be calculated and students can extend the task to consider angle sums of polygons.

This is a problem I have used on many occasions where different students have been able to develop the idea to different depths. Such a problem as this confirms for me the importance of finding tasks that promote the enrichment of mathematical thinking in contrast to 'accelerating' students' thinking . . . the depth of zooming in rather than the speed of zooming off I suppose!

How many triangles can be made with integer length sides that have a perimeter of 30cm?

This is quite a simple question and is, therefore, accessible for younger students. However, there are dangers lurking of either misinterpreting the question or of not taking into account the basic requirements pertaining to lengths of sides to form a triangle. For students to recognize that the two shorter lengths must total to a value greater than the longest side, is a considerably important piece of knowledge about forming any triangle . . . unless of course the triangle is isosceles in which case . . . or if the triangle is equilateral so that . . .

As we can see there are several complexities which we take for granted at our learners' peril! Indeed, I have seen older students begin work on this problem by writing out a list of triples all of which sum to 30, yet most of which don't form triangles, for example {1, 1, 28} and {1, 2, 27}, etc.

One approach might be to ask students to construct triangles using a compass, pencil and ruler. As different solutions are produced these can be instantly displayed so the task becomes one of: 'Have all the possible solutions been found?'

Extension ideas appear in Idea 47.

Some extension tasks to the problem in Idea 46 are:

1   Discuss conditions for forming triangles regarding edge lengths and write a list of values without actually constructing triangles. For example, with a perimeter of 30 the complete set (not counting rearrangements that will produce congruent triangles) contains between 15 and 25 solutions. The task is for students to create a systematic list to prove they have found them all.

2   Questions might also be posed about the types of triangles formed, for example: 'How many scalene, isosceles and equilateral triangles are there?' Scalene and isosceles triangles can be further classified according to whether they have three acute angles or one obtuse and two acute angles. A further question could be: 'Is there a right-angled triangle?'

3   What happens if order matters and congruent triangles are counted? For example, for any isosceles triangle there are three solutions and for any scalene triangle there will be six solutions.

4   Students in the upper KS4 and KS5 have a context for calculating angles and areas of triangles produced. Suppose a 'base' length is plotted on a coordinate grid so the end-points lie on grid points. How can the coordinates of the third point be calculated?

5   What happens if we remove the rule of integer values? Clearly there will be an infinite set of results, however, if students work with a fixed base length then the construction of the loci of an ellipse will not be too far away from realization.

6   By changing the size of the perimeter, students can explore how many triangles can be formed from different perimeters.

An interesting way to engage students in the production of the seven tangram pieces, shown below, is to give a sequence of verbal instructions and see if they can construct the final set of shapes. The following instructions might be used to begin this process:

o 'Draw a square ABCD'.
o 'Mark the mid-points of each side'.
o 'Join corner B to corner D'.
o 'Draw a line from the mid-point of line BD to corner C'.
o 'Join the mid-point of AB to the mid-point of AD', and so on.

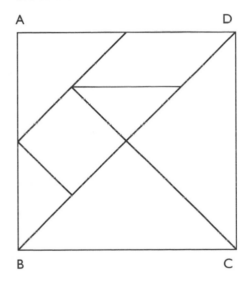

By describing the length of the small square piece as a (or 1) and the length of the large, overall square as b (or $2\sqrt{2}$), then areas and the perimeters of each individual shape can be defined (or calculated).

Students can try to find other 'simple' polygons, such as a right-angled isosceles triangle, a rectangle, a parallelogram and an isosceles trapezium. Once found, students can try to work out the perimeters of these shapes.

The following idea is written as a short article, by Jean Sauvy in the ATM journal *Mathematics Teaching* 114 and is about creating all the possible convex polygons (which means every internal angle is less than 180°).

Every one of the shapes below can be made each time from seven tangram pieces.

There are 13 such polygons and these are shown below.

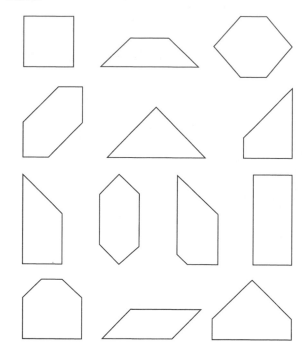

PROBLEM 1

Can students make them all?

PROBLEM 2

As they are made students can be asked to work out the perimeter of each one and then order them in terms of smallest to largest perimeter.

PROBLEM 3

Students can be asked to draw a scattergraph of length of longest diagonal against perimeter.

This idea could be used in the first instance to develop students' understanding of line symmetry and is based upon a visualization/mind imagery approach.

o Fold a square piece of paper in half through its vertical line of symmetry to form a rectangle.

o Cut off an isosceles right-angled triangle from the mid-point of the longest side of the folded piece of paper to one of the corners.

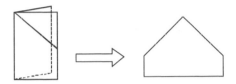

There are two possible ways of doing this; when the shapes are unfolded, one forms a pentagon with internal angles 90°, 135°, 90°, 135° and 90° (as shown above) and the other forms a pentagon with internal angles 90°, 45°, 270°, 45° and 90°.

As a visualization task students could be asked to make a sketch of the shapes they think will be formed by cutting off different corners before the outcome is revealed. This task can be developed in different directions and this will depend upon the main concepts we want students to work on. Some are:

o Producing tiling patterns from the different shapes formed.

o Calculating the angle sum of the shapes formed. Helping students make sense of the size of internal angles in concave polygons is an important concept here.

Carrying out a different number of folds before a corner is sliced off will produce different polygons, for example: by making a vertical and then a horizontal fold and cutting an isosceles right-angled triangle off forms an octagon; by folding into thirds with two vertical folds a concave hexagon is formed; by folding into quarters with two vertical folds, heptagons are formed.

Teaching students that *stuckness* is a state we all get into at times, and it should not be seen as a failure or shortcoming but instead as a positive state, is very important (Mason, Burton and Stacey, *Thinking Mathematically*, 1984). This is particularly the case if we are able to recognize our state of stuckness and look for alternative ways of working to become unstuck.

The following problem is one I have used to actively cause stuckness, which I tell students at the outset to encourage them to think of ways of getting unstuck rather than feeling there is no solution and, therefore, giving in.

The problem statement is:

'Dissect an obtuse-angled isosceles triangle into a finite number of acute-angled triangles using straight lines only.'
(Ascertaining that a 90° is neither acute nor obtuse is likely to be important information.)

There is no 'trickery' involved and the number of acute-angled triangles is finite and there is a rather neat geometrical solution.

This problem becomes very difficult very quickly and is, therefore, appropriate for higher attaining students in KS4 or for use in a KS5 classroom.

The problem is easy to pose yet not easy to solve and goes as follows:

o Draw a regular polygon.
o Mark the mid-point of each edge.
o Join adjacent pairs of points together to form a smaller regular polygon inside the original.

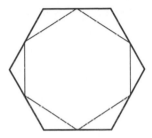

The problem is to find the area of the smaller polygon as a function of the area of the larger polygon.

With an equilateral triangle, the inner triangle will be ¼ of the area of the original. With a square, the inner square will be ½ the area of the original . . . with a pentagon . . .

PASSOLA

This idea requires some students to sit in a circle with their chairs equally spaced around a circle, a ball of string and a range of grid papers for recording purposes. These grids have different numbers of equally spaced dots arranged on the circumferences of circles.

The idea develops by holding onto the loose end of the ball of string then passing the ball a fixed number of spaces to someone else in the circle (this is the pass size). This person wraps the string around a finger then passes the ball to another person using the same pass size. This routine continues until the ball of string returns to the first person. At this point a shape, either a polygon, a straight line or a star shape will have been formed.

The outcome depends upon the number of people in the circle and the pass size rule applied. Clearly if there are 12 people in the circle and a pass size of four is used, the shape will be an equilateral triangle. If there are 12 people and a pass size of five is used, a 12-pointed star will be made.

The idea is to find what different shapes are made and how these relate to the number of people in the circle and the pass size used. Students might be encouraged to draw up a two-way table to explain what happens for different numbers of dots on the perimeter and the size of the pass rule.

The idea could be developed by asking students to calculate the angles of the vertices of the shapes produced (including star shapes).

Another development could be to calculate perimeters of the shapes (or the lengths of the lines forming star shapes).

One of the PGCE students I had the pleasure to work with last year, Jo Jeffrey, taught a lesson based upon loci I am keen to share. What was valuable about the lesson was how she adapted a people-loci approach (see *Getting the Buggers to Add Up*, Continuum 2004, pp. 53–54) to develop the basic concept of loci to one of using magnetic counters distributed to various students/volunteers throughout the lesson.

Jo asked each person holding a magnetic counter to come to the whiteboard and place their counters according to different conditions. Some of these were:

o Place your counter 20 cm away from the edge of the board (producing the loci of a pair of parallel lines).
o Place your counter an equal distance between two adjacent sides of the board (producing the loci of an angle bisector).
o Place your counter 20 cm away from a marked point on the board (producing the loci of a circle).
o Place your counter an equal distance between a given pair of points (producing the loci of a perpendicular bisector to a line joining the two initial points.

As students completed each task Jo asked them to make a sketch of the situation, ensuring they had access to the mathematical vocabulary associated with each loci produced, for example parallel lines, angle bisector, circle and perpendicular bisector.

Once students have gained the basic idea of what a loci is they can be challenged to construct other more complex loci, such as finding the set of points that are equidistant between:

o A line and a point (producing a parabola).
o A circle and a point (there are various scenarios here depending upon the position of the point both outside and inside the circle).

SQUARE CUT

Despite the title of this idea it has nothing to do with cricket. It is an idea I first met on a course to learn about counselling techniques; I have adapted the idea as an active and fun problem for the mathematics classroom.

Take five square pieces of card and dissect each into three pieces. Each dissection has to be different, although this does not mean that every one of the 15 resulting shapes will be different. For example, a square might be dissected into two right-angled trapeziums and a square as in the diagram below.

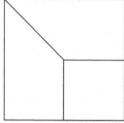

Using double-sided sellotape stick each of the fifteen pieces onto the backs of fifteen students; they cannot see their own piece but they can see each other's. The challenge is for students to form themselves into groups of threes so everyone forms part of a square.

If one is feeling particularly brave, you might have each set of shapes duplicated in two different colours, so a class of 30 students can try to solve the problem . . . however, we all have our different tolerance and risk-taking levels . . . where were those textbooks?

When two diagonals are cut from a regular pentagon, three isosceles triangles are formed; two of them are the congruent. One is a tall thin isosceles triangle (**T**) and another is a short squat isosceles triangle (**S**)

As a first task, students could be asked to work out the angles in each of these triangles. The next task is to make new shapes by joining together combinations of triangles **T** and **S**, full edge to full edge.

Fibonacci spotters may be able to use these shapes to make two alternating sets of isosceles triangles, generating the sequence 1, 1, 2, 3, 5, 8, . . . or using the symbols **T**, **S**, **TS**, **STS**, **TSSTS**, **STSTSSTS**, each of these combinations can be used to form enlargements of **T** and **S** type triangles.

The next idea is to explore diagonals in a hexagon. Here it is possible to cut off two different lengths of diagonals and there are three possible ways of dissecting a hexagon:

○ One dissection produces a rectangle and two isosceles triangles.
○ A second dissection produces an isosceles triangle, a scalene right-angled triangle and an isosceles trapezium.
○ A third dissection produces two isosceles triangles and a kite.

For each dissection what different shapes can be formed by rearranging the pieces?

How many different dissections are there by slicing two diagonals from a heptagon, an octagon, a nonagon, etc?

What are the sizes of the angles in the shapes formed by the different solutions?

To answer this question students will need a strategy for calculating the size of the external and, therefore, the internal angles in a regular polygon.

If the diagonals cross each other there will be even more possibilities and even more shapes to be played around with and explored.

FINDING SOME CENTRES OF TRIANGLES 1

These tasks can utilize or recycle those pieces of sugar paper or card where students have previously cut out a net of a shape right from the middle. The idea here is to cut the 'waste' up into different shaped triangles big enough to do some paper folding with.

THE INSCRIBED CENTRE

Take a triangle and fold each angle in half (this is, obviously, the process of bisecting each angle). Providing upon the accuracy of the folding (and the triangle-ness of the triangle), the three fold lines will intersect at a single point. This point is the centre of the inscribed circle which just touches the three sides of the triangle. Another way to describe this situation is the three sides of the triangle are tangents to a circle whose radii are perpendicular to the sides of the triangle.

THE CIRCUMSCRIBED CENTRE

We can find another centre of a triangle as follows. Ask students to join or fold together pairs of corners. Each of the three folds made becomes the perpendicular bisectors of the sides and again, accuracy allowing, these three lines will intersect at a single point which is the centre of a circle that just touches the three corners of the triangle; this is the circumscribed circle.

THE CENTRE OF GRAVITY

This centre is found by creating folds from the mid-point of each edge to each opposite angle. These three lines intersect at a point and this is the centre of gravity or the centroid; students might check their accuracy by trying to balance their triangle on the end of a pencil at this point of intersection.

The more traditional way of finding the inscribed and the circumscribed centres of triangles are to construct them using a compass (c), pencil (p) and a straight edge (se).

Helping students develop such construction skills is important and in the first instance requires them to practise and develop basic skills of angle and line bisection. There are other technical drawing type skills, such as forming triangles and dividing a line up into any number of equal segments that students can gain pleasure discovering and developing.

Using the more traditional p, c, se approach, alongside paper folding methods, as well as working within a dynamic geometry environment, such as *Cabri Géomètre*, are all important ways for learners to engage in geometric thinking.

Through p, c, se type construction students have opportunities to appreciate geometric properties of bisection and perpendicularity; these form the basis of further knowledge about circle and angle theorems and properties relating to tangents, radii, diameters and chords.

The problem below is one to challenge older students and through its solution students have opportunities to appreciate, or connect together, some of the skills associated with circle theorems and centres of triangles. The problem requires the following construction:

○ Draw a circle.
○ Mark three points A, B, C 'widely' (though not equally) spaced on the circumference.
○ Join these points together to form triangle ABC.
○ Draw tangents to the circle at each point A, B, C.
○ Where these tangents intersect each other (in pairs) mark points P, Q, R.

We now have two triangles, ABC and PQR. The challenge is to find relationships between the angles in triangle ABC and the angles in triangle PQR.

On a coordinate grid draw a quadrilateral in the first quadrant ensuring the four vertices lie on grid points.

Calculate the area of the quadrilateral; to do this students might dissect their shape into more easily 'work-out-able' pieces. Alternatively, they could be shown a method of framing the shape in a rectangle, working out the areas of the shapes outside the quadrilateral and within the rectangle, then subtracting the total from the area of the rectangle.

Now ask students to double each ordinate and plot the new shape. This will, of course, be an enlargement of the original quadrilateral with the origin as the centre of enlargement.

Calculate the area of the enlarged shape and compare with the area of the original. Try the same procedure again with other quadrilaterals.

What happens if the original shape is drawn across two, three or all four quadrants?

What happens to the area of the enlarged shape if the ordinates of the original are multiplied by 3 or by ½ or by 2½?

What happens to the shape if the original ordinates are multiplied by −2?

The three problems below are intended for students to 'play around' with coordinates in order to familiarize themselves with coordinate geometry.

In setting up each task there are, potentially, two important issues involved. The first is teacher expectation, that students are able to generate examples for themselves and each other. The second is ownership, of students developing a task without the teacher needing to prepare a worksheet.

PROBLEM 1

o Find the mid-point of a straight line segment between two points, for example (2, 5) and (6, 3).

o Do lots of examples choosing different pairs of starting points.

o Generalize for the mid-point between any two points P_1 and P_2.

o Check the generality holds when negative ordinates are used.

PROBLEM 2

o Draw some squares and write the coordinates of the corners of the square.

o Give your partner information about two points for each square; this might be a) a pair of adjacent points (in which case there will be two solutions), or b) a pair of diagonally opposite points (in which case there will be a unique solution).

o Partners then have to try to draw the squares from the information provided.

PROBLEM 3

In pairs, each student draws a pentagon with three right angles and one line of symmetry.

Students give their partner some information about their shape; the area of the pentagon and the coordinates of three of the corners. Partners then have to try to reproduce each other's pentagons.

These ideas build on Problem 2 described in Idea 60. The purpose is for students to see how the system of coordinates relates to the system of vectors.

PROBLEM 1

If P_1 and P_2 are adjacent corners of a square, find points P_3 and P_4 such that P_1, P_2, P_3 and P_4 form a square (there are two solutions to this problem).

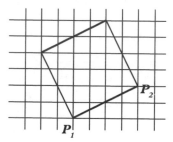

Examine the four vectors formed between pairs of adjacent corners of the square.

Try to generalize.

PROBLEM 2

If P_1 and P_3 are opposite corners of a square P_1, P_2, P_3, P_4, find points P_2 and P_4. Examine the vectors formed between opposite corners of the square and relate these to the vectors formed between adjacent corners. Try to generalize.

PROBLEM 3

Work out the area of a number of squares and write one of the vectors formed between a pair of adjacent corners for each square.

Look for a connection between the area and the chosen vector for each square. Try to generalize.

The general result is, of course, Pythagoras' theorem and though there is still much work to be done, i.e. to see the vector as the hypotenuse of a right-angled triangle, students will nevertheless be on the way towards making sense of the formula $a^2 + b^2 = c^2$.

Shapes A, B and C are each made by joining two right-angled isosceles triangles together. The joining 'rule' is placing sides of equal length together.

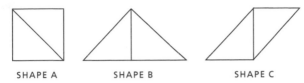

SHAPE A   SHAPE B   SHAPE C

This idea might begin by starting with a square and slicing this into two triangles along a diagonal. The two triangles can be used to form Shape B; by carrying out a rotation of one triangle Shape C can be formed.

The following questions/tasks might then be considered:

o What is the angle sum for each shape?
o What are the symmetries of the shapes?
o What is the perimeter of each shape? (This can either be written algebraically or in surd form; the latter requiring knowledge of Pythagoras' theorem.)
o How many shapes can be made with three triangles? How many for four triangles?
o Questions about angle sums, symmetries and perimeter can be similarly considered.
o Students can be challenged to construct a system to show (prove) they have found all possible shapes using, say, four triangles.
o How many shapes can be formed if, say, four equilateral triangles are used instead of four right-angled isosceles triangles?
o What happens if 30°, 60° or 90° triangles are used?

BIG triangle templates may be useful for display purposes.

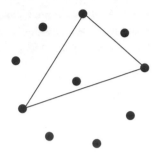

A circular geoboard is a piece of practical equipment with a certain number of equally spaced nails arranged on the circumference of a circle and one nail at the centre. There are, of course, an infinite number of circular geoboards depending upon how many pins there are around the circumference. Having a selection available with, say, 6, 7, 8, 9 and 10 pins around the circumference provides a rich vein of problems with opportunities to compare the different types of solutions for the problems described below.

Here I consider a circular geoboard with 9 equally spaced pins on the circumference (and one at the centre) and pose the problem of finding and recording as many 'different' (non-congruent) triangles whose vertices do not touch the centre pin.

If students are provided with ready marked-out grids on A4 paper this will save time when recording the shapes.

By asking a number of students to record one each of the shapes they have made on the board/screen there will be opportunities to:

o Classify the triangles.
o Discuss congruence.
o Describe the shapes.

One method I use to encourage students to give clear explanations is to ask them to describe the shape as 'over a telephone'. The reason for this is for students to use verbal instructions and to consider ways of coding the shapes made.

These discussion points can lead to students trying to prove they have found all the possible triangles.

Having tried to find, and prove they have found, all possible triangles on a 9-pin (plus one at the centre) geoboard, subsequent tasks can be:

1 What sizes are the angles of the triangles that have been produced?

o Whether this problem is utilized as a context for students to measure angles with a protractor or whether it is for students to use and apply knowledge of angle is dependent upon the teacher's intentions in the first instance. Of course it is feasible and perhaps desirable for both outcomes to occur.

o Seeking to solve this problem without using a protractor utilizes the centre pin; this is because we know that the angle size at the centre (between adjacent pins) is 40°. With this knowledge it is possible to work out angles of the triangles whose vertices lie on the circumference by drawing construction lines from the centre pin. The issue for the teacher is to decide whether (or when) to introduce the idea of using the centre pin as a way of calculating angles in the triangles.

2 How many triangles are there if we remove the condition of non-congruence?

3 How many non-congruent triangles can be made on geoboards with different numbers of pins at the circumference?

4 When triangles are made on geoboards with an even number of pins on the circumference, then right-angled triangles are going to appear in the set of solutions and this might be a preliminary stepping stone to angle in circle theorems.

CIRCULAR GEOBOARD 3

The next problem is aimed at developing students' knowledge of angle and circle theorems and for this purpose I suggest using a geoboard with an even number of pins on the circumference. This idea builds upon students knowing how to calculate the sizes of angles in triangles whose vertices lie at the circumference of the circular geoboard. Armed with this knowledge we can pose problems such as:

1 Make/draw all the triangles which have one side length that is common to each and find the size of the angle that is opposite to (or subtended from) this side (chord). This task is clearly aimed at students recognizing that angles subtended from a common chord are equal.

    o It is important to recognize that this and subsequent problems are 'only' demonstrating certain facts about angle/circle theorems; they are not proofs.

2 Make/draw some quadrilaterals whose vertices all lie on the circumference. These will be cyclic quadrilaterals and by examining the angles students can begin to recognize that opposite angles in a cyclic quadrilateral sum to 180°.

3 Make/draw some quadrilaterals where one of the vertices lies on the centre pin. This will produce two possible scenarios. If a 'chevron' shape is made then the outside angle at the centre will be twice the 'opposite' angle at the circumference. If any other quadrilateral is formed then there is another interesting connection to be found between the internal angle at the centre and the opposite angle at the circumference.

These problems will be best suited for either older students in the main or for high-attaining younger ones.

Returning to the triangles that have previously been made in Ideas 63, 64 and 65, one problem is to calculate and order by size the perimeter of each one. Whether (or if) students need to be reminded that it would be a 'good' idea to describe the length from the centre pin to any outside pin as unit length is clearly a decision for individual teachers to make. This problem will, however, demand that students use and apply their knowledge of trigonometry.

A further problem is to ask students to calculate the area of the triangles they have found and this will demand that students delve even deeper into their trigonometric knowledge banks.

Puzzles to see how your students *measure up*

Returning to a square 9-pin geoboard, just three non-congruent squares can be formed; the areas of the squares are 1, 2 and 4 (square units). By comparison to a 2-by-2 4-dot grid, two of the squares (having areas 2 and 4) could be considered 'new' squares.

How many 'new' squares, each with different areas, can be made on a 16-dot grid? What is the total number of squares that can be formed on a 16-dot grid?

By increasing the size of the geoboard what new squares and total number of squares can be formed?

Is it possible to predict the new and the total number of squares for successively larger square grids?

By comparing the areas of the squares with the problem about vectors in Idea 61, opportunities exist for students to engage in pre-Pythagoras concept formation.

So far all the problems described here and in Ideas 43 and 44 have been formulated in the 2D plane. Imagine a 3D geoboard . . . make up some problems of your own.

This idea provides students with opportunities to develop their understanding of the concept of the area of a rectangle beyond the simplistic, formulaic notion of 'length multiplied by width'.

The problem might also be used as a pre-Pythagoras task, as the solutions to the problem can later be related to Pythagoras' theorem.

The task is to find all the rectangles, on a square grid, with an area of 20cm^2 such that the corners of the rectangle always lie on a grid point.

There are three 'easy' solutions, i.e. a 1-by-20, a 2-by-10 and a 4-by-5. There are four more solutions, none of which are congruent rectangles to the three listed. One of the solutions is arrived at by the following calculation: $(1^2 + 3^2) \times 2$ or the sum of two square numbers multiplied by two . . . but what does the picture look like?

This idea could be used as a systematic attempt to sum square numbers.

The following areas will provide students much to think about: 50 cm^2, 72 cm^2, 90 cm^2 and 100 cm^2, each of which has a minimum of nine solutions.

A whole-class task could be to find all the possible solutions from 1 up to 100. To do this small groups of students could be given ten or a dozen different numbers between 1 and 100 to find all possible solutions; there could be some interesting display work to emerge.

This idea is for students to explore triangles with a constant area and one side length constant. The intention is to help them construct an understanding of the formula for the area of a triangle: $A = \frac{1}{2}bh$ or $A = \frac{bh}{2}$.

On 1 cm-square grid paper ask students to draw as many non-congruent triangles as possible, all of which have the same area of 6 cm^2 and a constant length of 4 cm.

Using A4 paper there will be more than a couple of dozen triangles that fit this criteria. Three of them, an isosceles, a scalene (acute angled) and a right-angled triangle will probably be the 'easiest' three to find. Students may need further encouragement to look for other triangles fitting the criteria, all of which have an obtuse angle.

Once a large collection of triangles have been found these can be made into an 'instant' display by sticking cut-outs of these triangles on a large sheet of sugar paper with each triangle orientated so the constant length (of 4 cm in this example) becomes the base of each triangle. This visual display is intended to reveal the observation that all the triangles have the same perpendicular height (of 3 cm).

By changing the length of the constant side to a different measure, such as 3cm, and keeping the constant area as 6 cm^2, then another display can be formed and this time the perpendicular height will always be 4 cm.

Students can explore what happens for triangles with different (constant) areas and constant base lengths.

This idea is based upon students exploring different types of triangles formed when surrounded by three squares. If the lengths of the squares provided measure from 3 cm to 17 cm, this will provide students with plenty of triangles to make.

Providing students with the resources (square pieces of card with lengths from 3 to 17 marked on) will obviously require careful preparation. However, once different size squares have been drawn on templates and these have been copied onto card, students can cut out squares, calculate the areas and write these on each square.

The idea is for students to choose three squares and use an edge of each square to form or 'surround' triangles. Because of the lengths chosen there will be many sets of three squares that will not form triangles; this can lead to students recognizing the condition of the total length of the two shorter sides needing be greater than the longest side in order to form a triangle.

The main point of the task is for students to explore lengths and, therefore, the areas of squares needed to make scalene triangles classified by:

o all acute angles;
o one obtuse angle;
o one right angle.

Because of the lengths used (from 3 to 17) between 200 and 250 scalene triangles can be formed; given just five of the triangles will be right-angled, students will have a substantial challenge to find these triangles. This lends itself to a whole class, working in groups, to systematically seek out the five right-angled solutions.

The main intention is to recognize the existence of following equations/inequalities based upon the areas of the squares and the following coding: S = smallest area, M = middle-size area and L = largest area.

o For all acute-angled triangles $S + M > L$.
o For obtuse-angled triangles $S + M < L$.
o For right-angled triangles $S + M = L$.

For students to make sense of the formula '$C = \pi d$', where C is the circumference and d is the diameter of a circle, it is not easy yet is most important. Indeed, sense-making of mathematics *per se* is fundamental to students becoming more confident and, therefore, more competent mathematicians. How students' understanding is formed, so they can use and apply the required knowledge to a range of situations, is equally important.

The idea I offer here is one I have used with some 'success' and is based upon students working with strips of scrap paper of different lengths. The idea works as follows:

○ Take a strip of paper and measure its length to the nearest millimetre.

○ Join the two ends together with sellotape without any overlap; the previous measure is now the circumference of the circle.

○ By rolling a finger of each hand around the inside of the strip form a shape as close as possible to a circle.

○ Measure the diameter of the circle; to do this students might take two or three measures to establish as accurate a measure as possible.

○ Record the two measures of diameter and circumference.

○ Repeat these steps for a number of different length strips.

Students can draw a graph of d against C, to help them recognize the connection between the two measures. By graphing the multiples of three on the same pair of axes, students may recognize a similarity between the two graphs.

The intention here is for students to become familiar with and form connections, both algebraically and graphically, between pairs of symbols C, d, r, and the constant π. I find the following questions can be useful.

How are d and r connected (i.e. $d = r \times 2$)?
What does the graph of r against d look like?

How are r and d connected?
What does the graph of d against r look like?

How are C and d connected?
What does the graph of d against C look like?

How are d and C connected?
What does the graph of C against d look like?

How are C and r connected?
What does the graph of r against C look like?

How are r and C connected?
What does the graph of C against r look like?

To calculate the area of a circle, again, teachers will have their favourite tasks. One approach I have found useful is to 'tell' students what the formula is and then ask them to gather data to try to verify the formula.

I ask students to draw a number of circles on 1cm-square paper, each with different radii, and count whole and part squares to gain approximate answers. Any radii between 2 cm and 10 cm can be chosen (on A4 paper) and if students are encouraged to use radii such as 3.8 cm or 6.2 cm, they can see how accurate their results are by comparison to applying the formula.

By adding the symbol A (area) to the earlier list, students can attempt to construct complex connections. With the four symbols r, d, C and A there are 12 pairs of connections (counting reverses), the most complicated perhaps being the connection between A and C.

A SURFACE AREA PROBLEM

I first met this idea in an ATM workshop with Barbara Ball. I have subsequently used the problem on many occasions.

Students will need access to linking cubes and isometric dot paper.

The idea is based upon making shape, initially, from linking cubes.

The problem uses 5, then 6, 7 and 8 cubes and considers what different surface areas are possible.

The value of this problem lies in the fact that students are likely to see a 'nice' pattern emerging based upon shapes made from 5, 6 and 7 cubes. However, when 8 cubes are made a 'hole' appears in the data and this is, I feel, a useful way of demonstrating to students that mathematics does not always follow nice neat patterns.

There is, of course, an explanation about why the hole appears in the data with 8 cubes and inviting students to try to explain why this happens will be a suitable challenge.

This idea is taken from *Inclusive Mathematics 11–18*, (Continuum, 2002, pp. 117–18).

Using 2cm-square grid paper ask students draw a dozen or so right-angled triangles, keeping, in the first instance, to the grid lines.

Students then complete a table as below, where the angles are measured with a protractor.

Opposite length	adjacent length	Measured angle	The ratio *o:a* as a fraction	The ratio *o:a* as a decimal
5	2	68°	$^5/_2$	2.5
1	3	18°	$^1/_3$	0.333
3	4	37°	$^3/_4$	0.75
3	2	56°	$^3/_2$	1.5
etc.	etc.	etc°.	etc.	etc.

Students can share information, perhaps by several people writing their answers on the board/screen to provide opportunities for observation and discussion.

Once plenty of information is available students can rearrange the data in terms of angle sizes going from smallest to largest.

Further questions are:

o What happens to the ratio between the 'opposite' and 'adjacent' sides as the angle increases?
o What happens to the angle as the ratio increases?
o What is special about those angles where the ratio is 1?
o Can we find an angle whose ratio is −1?
o What happens as the measured angle approaches 90°?
o What happens to the ratio for angles greater than 90° and less than 180°?
o What does the graph of angle plotted against the decimal ratio look like?

A few beer MATs, some glue and a lot of imagination

An amazing resource, sold by the ATM, www.atm.org.uk and created by Adrian Pinel, are 2-D 'beer' MATs. These are, in the main, regular polygons with a common edge length and this property makes MATs highly suitable for producing 2D tessellation designs. This in turn can lead to students classifying tessellations and working out internal angles of polygons.

The main use of MATs is to make 3D solids and, together with small amounts of Copydex glue, all kinds of solids can be created.

The first idea I offer is based upon students working only with equilateral triangle and square MATs in the first instance. The intention behind this restriction is to create an opportunity for students to explore a problem, of finding convex-angled solids, within specific parameters.

As solids emerge students can:

○ Attempt to name them.
○ Count how many Faces (F), Vertices (V) and Edges (E) each has.
○ Seek the connection between F, V, and E or Euler's Rule ($F + V = E + 2$).

With equilateral triangle MATs three of the five Platonic solids can be made (tetrahedron, octahedron and icosahedron). Using the square MAT students can easily produce a cube (or a hexahedron) which is another Platonic solid. (To gain the complete set of five Platonic solids students will need to use twelve pentagon MATs to make a dodecahedron.)

Asking students to prove there are just five Platonic solids will provide a suitable challenge.

There are more solids to be made using combinations of square and equilateral triangle MATs, for example a triangular prism, a square-based anti-prism and a cuboctahedron which is made from six squares and eight equilateral triangles.

This is a development of the ideas suggested in Idea 75. A further rich area for exploration is to find all the different convex-angled solids, using triangular MATs only. There is a finite set and these are called deltahedra, and as before, three of these are Platonic solids: the tetrahedron, octahedron and icosahedron. The challenge is for students to find the remaining deltahedra.

This holds an interesting mathematical 'blip' which occurs when Faces, Vertices and Edges are counted for each deltahedra, resulting in a 'missing' set of values in what appears initially to be a straightforward sequence. The names of the remaining five deltahedra are anything other than straightforward! However, salvation is at hand in *Mathematical Models* by H.M. Cundy and A.P. Rollett (Clarendon Press, 1952, pp. 135, 136).

A further challenge is for students to examine the symmetries of the 'non-Platonic' deltahedra; a task that will keep the highest attaining mathematicians engaged.

A further idea is for students to explore the relationship between the tetrahedron and the octahedron. KS4 or KS5 students can be posed the problem of calculating the dihedral (or the solid) angles, between pairs of faces, for these solids. This will require students to solve a problem in 3D using trigonometry.

For younger students there is an opportunity for them to see a combination of tetrahedrons and the octahedrons fill 3D space. This can lead to some interesting shapes being created and for the possibility of creating a 3D 'mobile' display.

This task is developed in the final part of Idea 84.

This idea is for students to explore truncations of solids.

Basically, there are two different types of truncations that can be created. One is to slice off the vertices of a solid through the mid-point of the edges between each vertex. The other is to slice off the vertices through a point *somewhere* between the vertex and the mid-point (for example, one third of the distance down each edge).

This idea is for students to explore the truncations of the five Platonic solids, i.e. the tetrahedron, hexahedron, octahedron, icosahedron and dodecahedron. This would be a useful small group task. As students explore truncations some amazing results are waiting to be to found.

One way for students to truncate solids is to physically cut off the vertices; this however can be messy and possibly risky (in terms of health and safety). My preferred approach is to ask students to visualize, in the first instance, what shapes are formed by truncating. Another approach is to draw construction lines. For example, by truncating a tetrahedron about the mid-point of each edge an octahedron (surprisingly) is formed.

By truncating either a hexahedron and an octahedron about the mid-point of each edge a cuboctahedron is formed. This is also one of the 13 Archimedean solids and these are developed in Idea 78.

Students can explore the following questions:
○ What different solids emerge?
○ What happens when Euler's rule is applied?
○ What is the connection between the Faces, Vertices and Edges of a solid and the different truncations so formed? Is it possible to predict results?

Asking students to try to find and construct all the possible 13 Archimedean solids would be a substantial challenge. To help students engage in such a task they will first of all need to know how an Archimedean solid is defined (i.e. they are formed from more than one regular polygon and at every vertex the same type and number of regular polygons meet). For example, with the cuboctahedron, two equilateral triangles and two squares meet at each vertex.

There are also two infinite sets of Archimedean solids that students could be introduced to, i.e. the set of prisms and the set of anti-prisms. This idea focuses on the finite set of 13.

Students could be told what shapes are required to form them, i.e:

- Equilateral triangles
- Squares
- Regular pentagons
- Regular hexagons
- Regular octagons
- Regular decagons

If further information is considered useful, say for younger students, they could be told the combinations of polygons required to make the solids, i.e:

- Triangles and squares (to form three Archimedean solids)
- Triangles and pentagons (two solids)
- Triangles and hexagons (one solid)
- Triangles and octagons (one solid)
- Triangles and decagons (one solid)
- Squares and hexagons (one solid)
- Pentagons and hexagons (one solid)
- Triangles, squares and pentagons (one solid)
- Squares, hexagons and octagons (one solid)
- Squares, hexagons and decagons (one solid)

Several of these solids are likely to have already been created from the various truncations carried out in Idea 77. As these are made students might be told these solids are Archimedean.

Questions about calculating the surface area of the solids and the volumes of the solids will provide the most confident mathematicians with some really 'hard sums' to do!

This idea is about making two open cuboids and comparing volumes. This idea is also described in the ATM publication *Learning and Teaching Mathematics without a Textbook*.

The task described below can be simplified by using rectangular pieces of paper that have integer length dimensions.

Take one piece of A4 paper and fold it into four equal strips, 'landscape' orientation. Make this into an open, top and bottom, cuboid.

Fold the other piece of A4 paper into four equal strips 'portrait' orientation and make a second cuboid.

What are the volumes of each cuboid?

Further questions might be:

○ What is the percentage volume decrease between the largest and the smallest cuboids?

○ What is the percentage volume increase between the smallest and the largest cuboids?

○ Suppose tops and bottoms are added to each cuboid, what are the surface areas of each?

○ If we use any size of rectangular paper, say *l* by *w*, can the surface areas in the previous question be written in terms of *l* and *w*?

○ What volumes are gained if we make each piece of paper into triangular prisms?

○ What volumes are gained if we make each piece of paper into cylinders?

TAKE AN A4 PIECE OF PAPER

This problem is one I have used dozens of times and recently began talking about during a meal with some mathematics advisors . . . a typical meal-time conversation when mathematicians get together! I was intrigued to see just how challenging the problem became and how keen my colleagues were to ascertain the 'right' answer.

The question is again simple to pose yet holds hidden complexities. I might wish to use the problem as a mind-imagery task or I might want students to make the solids under consideration and use the models to work on the task. I might do both of these, starting with an imagery problem and later allowing students to use solids. My initial question is:

'How many planes of symmetry does a cube (or a hexahedron) have?'

I want students to explain where planes of symmetry slice through the cube and describe the cross-sectional shapes formed by different planes of symmetry.

Further questions can be:

○ What planes of symmetry does an octahedron have?
○ What connections exist between the planes of symmetry of a cube and the planes of symmetry of an octahedron?
○ Where are the axes of rotational symmetry of a cube and what is the order of rotational symmetry for each axis?
○ Where are the axes of rotational symmetry of an octahedron and what is the order of rotational symmetry for each axis?

Making the solids and showing what cross-sectional shapes are formed, and using straws to show axes of rotational symmetry, can provide students with interesting challenges.

Drawing 3D shapes on isometric paper is a skill some students can do intuitively while others require careful instructions to help them become confident. We might make good use of the teaching strategy of students who 'can' helping those who 'cannot', however, being able to represent 3D shapes in a 2D picture is only a means to an end. Providing students with problems where drawing diagrams may help in the solution is more important.

One is to give students just four linking cubes and ask them to find all the different shapes by joining them together and to draw the different solutions they find. Discounting rotations there are less than a dozen possible solutions.

This simple-to-pose problem has several aspects; further questions can be raised such as:

o What does 'different' mean in relation to the shapes made?
o What symmetries does each shape possess?
o What different surface areas are there for the shapes?
o Can students prove they have found a complete set of shapes?

If a whole-class approach to the last question is felt to be desirable, this problem might be a useful context for engaging all the students in discussions about the notion of proof. One approach might be to invite individuals to draw their solutions on the screen/board and use this collection of results to discuss how a proof about completeness might be developed.

AN ALTERNATIVE 'NET' OF A CUBE

Sometimes I want to provide a class with a 'closed' puzzle designed to grab interest and give them something to think about. The following is one such problem and is no more than a one-off type idea.

1 Divide a square piece of card equally into nine small squares arranged in a 3-by-3 square.
2 Cut through from any one of the lines that go from the edge towards the middle.
3 Continue the cut made in 2) and cut out the centre square.
4 Throw this centre square away.
5 You now have a shape with eight squares in a 'ring' separated by one cut.
6 Score all the remaining seven joins between the eight remaining squares.

The challenge is to form a cube by folding up the eight squares.

There is more than one solution.

A more complex task is for students to explain verbally or diagrammatically how the problem can be solved. To record different solutions students might code all the squares on one side as 1, 2, . . . 8 and all the squares on the other side as A, B, . . . H.

Asking students to explain to someone at home how the puzzle can be solved would be a worthy challenge and a useful homework task.

This idea is to dissect a cube into four congruent equilateral triangular-based pyramids and a tetrahedron.

To follow the instructions it may be useful to have a cube placed in front of you with the eight corners labelled 1 (top left-hand corner), 2, 3 and 4 moving anti-clockwise around the top face, then 5, 6, 7, 8 moving anti-clockwise around the bottom face. This means corner 1 is above corner 5, corner 2 is above corner 6, etc.

The apexes of the four pyramids are going to be four of the eight corners of the cube, for example corners 1, 3, 6 and 8.

Each pyramid is similarly constructed. As an example, the pyramid whose apex is at corner 1 is formed as follows: draw a line, diagonally from corner 4 to 2 and from 2 to 5 (and then back to corner 4). These three lines sketch out an equilateral triangle and form the base of one of the pyramids.

The idea is for students to construct four such pyramids and one tetrahedron so the bases of the (four) pyramids become the four faces of the tetrahedron.

The pyramids and the tetrahedron can now be put together to form a cube.

Two other cube dissections are described in *Getting the Buggers to Add Up* (Continuum, 2004, pp. 29–30).

This idea is a development of Idea 83 and is based upon the construction of eight equilateral triangle-based pyramids to form two cubes, each with a tetrahedron-shaped hole inside. These eight pyramids will form a regular octahedron and students can see, again, how the cube (hexahedron) and the octahedron are related.

An alternative to having each of the eight pyramids as separate solids is to hinge them together in two lots of four, each one being formed by hinging three pyramids around the three edges of a fourth pyramid. Each of these structures form hollow cubes when turned one way around, yet when they both are unfolded and turned back on themselves, the two shapes will join together to form an octahedron – amazing really.

As well as delighting in the marvel of this construction, students can construct formulae for the volumes of the different solids formed using C = Cube, T = tetrahedron, P = Pyramid and O = Octahedron, i.e.:

o $T + 4P = C$
o $8P = O$
o $2C - 2T = O$

Furthermore if we construct four (congruent) tetrahedrons and place these on four of the eight faces of the octahedron, a bigger tetrahedron can be formed. This tetrahedron will have a volume which is eight times the volume of the smaller tetrahedron. With this information the following formula emerges:

$8T = O + 4T$, so $O = 4T$.

Using this information the volumes of the solids can be compared with that of the cube.

SFGs, not perhaps as interesting as *The BFG* but nevertheless some giant-sized ideas for the classroom

EXTENDING SEQUENCES BACKWARDS

There are many instances of exercises where students are either asked to fill in the missing numbers or to extend a sequence by a given number of terms. An extension of this is to extend sequences backwards as well as forwards.

Extending linear sequences backwards provides a context for students to work with negative numbers. For example, by extending the sequence 4, 7, 10, 13, 16 backwards by five terms we have 16, 13, 10, 7, 4, _, _, _, _, _, leading to the values, 16, 13, 10, 7, 4, 1 −2, −5, −8, −11.

By extending a quadratic sequence backwards, students can see the symmetry involved. For example, taking the quadratic sequence 1, 3, 6, 10, 15 backwards by five terms produces, 10, 6, 3, 1, 0, 1, 3, 6, 10, 15.

Extending the Fibonacci sequence backwards by several terms produces 13, −8, 5, −3, 2, 1, 0, 1, 1, 2, 3, 5, 8, 13. An interesting oscillation occurs.

What happens when we extend the numbers 1, 3, 4, 7, 11 from the Lucas sequence backwards?

What happens when we extend powers of two backwards?

Suppose we make up a sequence based upon two values of a and b, where to find the next value in the sequence we calculate $2a + b$. So a sequence starting with 2 and 3 creates the following: 2, 3, 7, 13, 27, 53 ... What happens when we reverse this sequence? Suppose the rule was 2a − b?

This idea is based upon the knowledge that a linear sequence is 'nothing other' than a positive or a negative shift from an ordered list of multiples (commonly known as a multiplication 'table').

For example, the sequence 7, 11, 15, 19, 23 . . . is similar to the sequence 4, 8, 12, 16, 20 . . . The only difference is each term of the first sequence is three more than each number in the second sequence.

As the second sequence is multiples of four, the first sequence must be multiples of four plus three.

A further conceptual leap is for learners to appreciate that if the general term for the second sequence of numbers is $4n$, then the general term for the first sequence is $4n + 3$.

A task to help students practise and consolidate this knowledge is to set up a situation that works in reverse, where students set up questions and ask a partner to find solutions. The idea works as follows:

o Each student writes several lists of multiples, for example 5, 10, 15, 20, 25 . . .

o They also write the general term for each sequence, for example $5n$.

o For each sequence students add or subtract constant values, for example, by subtracting 2 from each number in the sequence we gain 3, 8, 13, 18, 23 . . . Again students write the general term for each sequence they create, for example, $5n - 2$.

o Students then swap their lists of sequences and have to work out the general terms for each sequence they are presented with.

o Students can self-check each other's answers.

This situation is ripe for students to draw graphs by making each sequence into a list of coordinate pairs and seeing for themselves the pairs of graphs create parallel lines.

EXPLORING LINEAR SEQUENCES

Finding opportunities for students to see concepts emerge in different contexts, and see how concepts are connected together in different ways, is necessary if mathematics is to be perceived as a coherent discipline.

This idea is initially aimed at the upper KS2–lower KS3 age range and will require students to have access to a simple (non-scientific) calculator and connects together concepts of factors and drawing graphs.

Choose a number that has several pairs of factors, for example, 24.

Write these pairs of factors as coordinate pairs, i.e. (1, 24), (2, 12), (3, 8), (4, 6), (6, 4), (8, 3), (12, 2), (24, 1).

By plotting these points on a graph and joining them together with a smooth curve, students will effectively drawing the graph of $y = 24/x$.

An extension is to consider values that are not divisors of 24, for example 5, 7, 9. By examining the graph to see what the missing ordinates are in each coordinate pair (5, ?), (7, ?) etc, students can see how accurate, or otherwise, their readings are. Once the missing ordinates have been determined (within degrees of accuracy provided by the graph), students can check how close they are by multiplication [$5 \times 4.8 = 24$] and/or by division [$24 \div 5 = 4.8$].

Students will have departed from working with whole number solutions at this point. However, the key issue is that all the points between whole number coordinate pairs continue to produce points on the graph.

When are the two dimensions equal? This question could be used as a task in its own right and is aimed at students making sense of the concept of a square root, particularly if different degrees of accuracy are searched for prior to directing any of the students to the existence of the √ key.

What does the graph look like for a starting value other than 24?

What happens if graphs for different starting values are drawn on the same pair of axes?

This is a 'practise and consolidation' idea and requires students to learn the 'mechanics' of multiplying out expressions in pairs of brackets. Teachers will have different ways of explaining this, although my preferred approach is to use a two-way grid method as for multiplying numbers greater than ten together.

Inviting students to work in pairs may prove useful. Provide students with sheets of A3 or sugar paper.

Ask them to draw a line down the middle of their sheet (portrait orientation) and write their name(s) at the top of each half.

On the left-hand side of the line they write a number of pairs of factorized expressions, for example $(x + 2)(x + 5)$.

Sarah and Tom	Sarah and Tom
$(x + 2)$ $(x + 5)$	$x^2 + 7x + 10$

Using whatever method they know/have been taught, they work out the expansion of their expression, for example, $x^2 + 7x + 10$ and write this on the other side of the line.

Students could do a lot of these. I suggest they start with easy expressions and gradually write harder ones, i.e. starting with factors involving (+ and +), then (+ and −) or (− and +), then (− and −) with the x terms having a coefficient of 1.

Each person now has a number of factorized expressions on the left-hand side of their paper and the equivalent expansions on the right-hand side. Next they cut their sheet down the dividing line and swap their expanded expressions with another person. Pairs now try to work out what the factorizations are for each expression. Students subsequently check their answers with one another.

While resources such as graphical calculators and function graph plotting computer programs are marvellous tools to aid learning, I also want students to experience graphs by drawing them from first principles, by working out input, output values or $(x, f(x))$ and seeing for themselves how a graph illustrates a function. As students gain competence and confidence at graphing functions then using more sophisticated technology seems to be a logical next step to help them deepen their knowledge.

This idea, therefore, is based upon students exploring a range of connected functions that all have a coefficient of 1 for the x^2 term. The first task is for students to work in pairs to produce some display materials which will, in turn, act as a stimulus for discussion.

○ Provide pairs of students with an A3 sheet of square grid paper showing a pair of axes and the function $f(x) = x^2$ drawn in a thick felt-tip pen.

○ Ask them to plot the following graphs, each on a separate sheet of paper:

$f(x) = x^2 + 2$

$f(x) = x^2 - 2$

$f(x) = (x + 2)^2$

$f(x) = (x - 2)^2$

$f(x) = (x + 2)^2 + 2$

$f(x) = (x + 2)^2 - 2$

$f(x) = (x - 2)^2 + 2$

$f(x) = (x - 2)^2 - 2$

It does not matter if some pairs of students do more than others (this is one aspect of differentiated learning), what is important is being able to gather together enough information to form an instant display. I develop this in Idea 90.

This idea follows on from Idea 89 where a display has been created. By gathering students around the display they can be encouraged to discuss the similarities and the differences between the graphs and explore how they are related to the functions the students have plotted.

Because the coefficient of the x^2 term is always 1, then each graph will obviously have the same shape but will be positioned differently on the grid.

Other valuable information, in terms of analysing the graphs, is where the line of symmetry lies; again this information can be connected to the function under discussion.

Discussing how each of the graphs is a vector translation of $y = x^2$ is a development of this work, and determining how the vector translation relates to the corresponding function is a further complexity to consider.

A further development is for students to predict what happens if the graph is: $y = x^2 + 3$, or $y = (x - 3)^2$, etc.

Seeing what happens when the coefficient of the x^2 term becomes -1 will provide students with plenty to think about and try to make sense of.

So far students have been exploring quadratic graphs as transformations of $y = x^2$.

A next step could be to classify graphs in terms of whether they have two, one or no real roots.

Determining how real roots can be calculated is a further development and this is described in Idea 92.

Having considered quadratics where the coefficient of the x^2 term is 1, this idea is intended to develop students' thinking by considering coefficients of the x^2 term as something other than 1 (or −1). To try to achieve this the same procedure as described in Idea 89 – of asking pairs of students to work together to produce graphs on sheets of A3 paper which have $y = x^2$ graph already drawn on it – could be utilized.

Graphs for students to draw might be:

$y = 2x^2$

$y = 2x^2 - 3$

$y = 2x^2 + 3$

$y = 2x^2 + x - 3$

$y = 2x^2 + x + 3$

$y = 2x^2 - x - 3$

$y = 2x^2 - x + 3$

$y = \frac{1}{2}x^2$

$y = \frac{1}{2}x^2 - 3$

$y = \frac{1}{2}x^2 + 3$

$y = \frac{1}{2}x^2 + x - 3$

$y = \frac{1}{2}x^2 + x + 3$

$y = \frac{1}{2}x^2 - x - 3$

$y = \frac{1}{2}x^2 - x + 3$

Once students have produced sufficient graphs to form a display they can again gather around their work to discuss and analyse similarities and differences. The key aspects of this task are to recognize how the graphs compare to each other and to $y = x^2$.

This idea is a development from the previous four ideas; in my scheme of work these five ideas formed the basis for a module lasting three to four weeks.

The idea is based upon an exploration of real roots and the turning point for quadratics of the form:
$y = ax^2 + bx + c$ where a, b and c are in the range -4 to 4.

I would certainly encourage the use of graphical calculators or a computer graph plotting program; this is because I want students to start to examine what the real roots are, if any exist, together with the turning point, for graphs of quadratic functions. I also want students to systematically gather a lot of information for purposes of analysis.

This idea, therefore, is to encourage students to form systematic collections of families of graphs in order to see where the real roots and the turning point occurs, and how these are connected to the line of symmetry on a quadratic graph.

To enable students to work systematically I would suggest they initially restrict the coefficients (and the constant term) to values of -4, 3, -2, -1, 0, 1, 2, 3 and 4; this will provide them with plenty to have a go at.

The most confident students might be able to construct a procedure for predicting whether a function will have two, one or no real roots and where these real roots are. I expect some students to be capable of constructing a procedure for determining the turning point. At what point any teacher might decide to offer students procedures such as completing the square or 'the' quadratic formula will of course vary.

Ideas for budding data handlers

Making use of a daily newspaper weather page is an excellent resource for teaching mathematics and was suggested to me by Anne Watson during an informal chat at an ATM conference. I have used this resource with great success in my teaching over the years and this was a fantastic example of teachers' sharing ideas and engaging in professional development.

These are some reasons for students to use the weather page:

○ It contains a massive amount of 'real' and current information.
○ It provides opportunities for students to work with a range of areas for *Handling Data*, again using 'real' information.
○ It provides opportunities for cross-curricular work.

The first two ideas only require students to have access to one day's information. The last three require students to access a large number of different days' information so collecting the weather page over several weeks will be necessary for ideas 3, 4 and 5.

1 Draw a Centigrade to Fahrenheit conversion using the data from all over the world.
2 From the data of around Britain draw grouped frequency graphs for some of the following:
   ○ Number of sunshine hours.
   ○ Rainfall (in inches).
   ○ Highest temperature.
   ○ Lowest temperature.
   ○ Find the average highest and lowest temperatures.
   ○ Draw scattergraphs of highest against lowest temperatures.
3 Draw graphs of sunrise times for some of the places given (Belfast, Birmingham, etc). Why do different places have different amounts of daylight?
4 Draw graphs of moonset and moonrise
5 Graph high-tide times and low-tide times for various places around Britain.

This idea was first introduced to me in 1975 by Eric Love, my first head of department. It is based upon setting out three or four 'different' experiments, according to class-size, using cards, coins, dice and cubes. Each experiment is set out twice around the classroom. All experiments have the same probability outcomes. In groups of fours, students move simultaneously from one experiment to the next every five or so minutes.

If there are 'spare' bodies, they can help with data collection or dealing cards (see below).

Each experiment will require:

o An explanation sheet.
o Necessary equipment.
o Recording sheets.

The recording sheets are axes drawn on 1 cm-squared paper; the *spaces* on the horizontal axis are marked out 0, 1, 2, 3 and 4 and the *lines* on the vertical axis are marked 0 to 25.

Each experiment requires several sheets. Students record the outcomes of experiments they do and fill in data sheets continuously from where the previous group left off.

A sheet is considered 'full' when one column reaches the top.

The experiments are:

1 Each person is dealt a card from a 'pack' containing just eight cards containing four aces. Record whether 0, 1, 2, 3 or 4 aces are dealt.
2 Each person has a coin and these are spun simultaneously. Record whether 0, 1, 2, 3 or 4 heads appear.
3 Each person has a dice and these are thrown simultaneously. Record whether 0, 1, 2, 3 or 4 even numbers appear.
4 Each person takes a cube from a bag containing a lot of cubes, half of which are Red. Record whether 0, 1, 2, 3 or 4 red cubes appear.

As recording sheets are completed they can be collected in and stored for the next lesson.

This idea follows on directly from Idea 94 and is about students collating, re-recording, analysing and interpreting the data.

Small groups of students are provided with recording sheets, each with data from one of the experiments (1, 2, 3 and 4) carried out in the previous lesson. Each group totals up the frequencies of the five outcomes, i.e. 0, 1, 2, 3 and 4, from all the sheets for one of the experiments.

The important issue is that all four experiments eventually have a single set of results to show how frequently the outcomes of 0, 1, 2, 3 and 4 occurred.

Each of the four experiments can be illustrated with a block graph and groups can analyse and interpret the information. The expected outcomes 'should' approximate to the fifth line of Pascal's Triangle, i.e. 1, 4, 6, 4, 1 and as fractional amounts this becomes: $\frac{1}{16}$, $\frac{4}{16}$, $\frac{6}{16}$, $\frac{4}{16}$ and $\frac{1}{16}$, or 0.0625, 0.25, 0.375, 0.25 and 0.0625.

This knowledge, of how the lines of Pascal's Triangle relate to probability outcomes, would be too complex for most KS3 students. However, older students in KS4 and KS5 can use such data to work on these concepts. For younger students, just to be able to see how the results are distributed, and how these can be turned into decimal values and placed on a probability line (from 0 to 1) would provide useful mathematical insights.

This is a logical-thinking type task I have used many times and one that provokes much 'heated' debate. I was, therefore, heartened to see the same problem appear in Mark Haddon's *The Curious Incident of the Dog in the Night-time*, and readers of the book will recognize this problem.

The problem is based upon a quiz show where there are three doors. Behind one door is a marvellous prize, behind the other two doors are 'booby' prizes.

The idea works as follows:

1 The contestant is presented with three options to choose from.
2 Having made a choice the quiz show presenter then looks at the two options *not* chosen and discards one that would not have been a winner. This procedure is explained to the contestant.
3 The presenter then asks the contestant if s/he would like to change her/his mind and a) choose the remaining option, or b) stick with the original choice.

This is the crux point of the problem and although it seems illogical, the contestant doubles their chance of winning by changing her/his mind.

Having gone through the 'usual' heated debate about the seeming nonsense that changing one's mind doubles the possibility of winning, students could be encouraged to find ways of analysing the situation and proving how this problem works. One way is to draw a tree-diagram and consider what the different probabilities are at both stages of the procedure.

GUESS THE COLOUR

For this idea there are opportunities for students to work on the following:

o Comparing theoretical and experimental outcomes.
o Connecting fractions, decimal and percentages.
o Rounding results to a given number of decimal places.
o Understand how the probability of a (single) event increases as choice decreases.
o Carrying out an experiment several times means experimental data is more likely to match theoretical outcomes.

I have used this with 11- and 12-year-old students and it can easily be simplified for younger students.

Each student is given the same set of six differently coloured counters or linking cubes and asked to choose one counter/cube. I now take one counter/cube from a bag and see how many people in the class made the same choice of colour. This result is recorded in a two-way table as *Guess 1, Game 1*.

Everyone now removes this colour from their set of six, thus leaving them with five remaining colours to choose from. The procedure is repeated a further five times and each time results are recorded in the two-way table – *Guess 2, Game 1* then *Guess 3, Game 1*, etc. Clearly when there is only one colour to choose from, at guess 6, there should be a 100 per cent success rate; discussing the notion of certainty might be useful here.

Theoretically, the number of correct guesses should increase, however this may not be the case as we only have one data set. Playing a further five or so games, recording the values in the table and accumulating the number of correct outcomes from guess 1 through to guess 6 is likely to create a set of results closer to theoretical outcomes. Once a larger data set has been collated, results can be accumulated and analysed to compare experimental outcomes with theoretical outcomes.

The task, therefore, is about changing probabilities, from ⅙ (0.1667 or approximately 17%), to ⅕ (0.2 or 20%), . . . to ¼ with students experiencing this in a practical, active way working as a whole-class group.

Having a smaller number of different colours in the original set will simplify this task.

CAN YOU 'REACH' YOUR HEIGHT?

This idea is to consider how a person's arm span (reach) compares to their height and requires two measures to be taken, height (h) and arm span (s), (i.e. the length from left-hand finger tip to right hand finger-tip).

To use this idea I would prepare several tape measures placed both horizontally, approximately at students' ('average') shoulder height, and vertically around the room. This is so students can take the two measures as soon as they enter the room and the results can be written on the board/screen in a table of results.

By making a scatter graph of h against s students can see how spans and heights compare and the following questions might typically be posed: .

o How many people in the class are taller than their spans?
o How many people are wider than their height?
o Within a 5 per cent range, how many people have a span equal to their height?
o What percentage range would we need for half the people in the room to have a span equal to their height?

Other comparative measures could be:

o Height.
o Distance around head (around forehead and across the top of your ears).
o Length of smallest finger.
o Hand span.
o Length from wrist to elbow.

Each of these measures will provide plenty of opportunities for students to work on:

o Different types of averages.
o The 'most average' person in a class.
o The range.
o Grouped frequency graphs.
o Scattergraphs.
o Whether approximate ratios exist between pairs of measures, for example does an approximate ratio exist between distance around head compared to height?

CUBES IN AN ENVELOPE

This is a probability-based task and is about trying to predict the proportion of an 'unknown' data set through sampling. The task requires A4 envelopes and linking cubes.

Cubes of two or three different colours are placed in each envelope and on the front I write the total number of cubes the envelope contains and a letter to code/ identify it. For example, an envelope marked '10 cubes' and 'A', could contain seven green and three white cubes, an envelope marked '9 cubes' and 'B' might contain four red, three yellow and two blue cubes, etc.

I set up the following procedure using, for example, envelope 'A'. I ask each student in turn to remove one cube, call out the colour and replace it, taking care not to look inside the envelope.

I ask a volunteer to record the number of cubes and the colour on the board. After approximately half the students have each drawn and replaced a cube I ask the recorder to tally up the totals in reference to the data now collected. I ask everyone else to make a prediction of what they think the proportion of colours of cubes is in the envelope.

The experiment continues until everyone has had a turn and again I ask everyone to make a second prediction or to stick with the original one. I shall ask some individuals to say what predictions they have made and try to justify their results by explaining how the data has influenced their thinking.

Finally I empty out the answer to reveal the contents of the envelope.

Students then carry out further experiments in pairs using different envelopes. I ensure there are sufficient envelopes for each pair plus two or three extras. This means students can (and will) work at different speeds.

An approach to testing I have found useful, for a number of reasons, is one where I invite students to write test questions, say for an end-of term assessment. The method works as follows.

At the beginning of a lesson two or three weeks from an end of term I review the different topic areas a class has worked on. This might involve asking students to try to remember what each topic has been about, and to do this they might work in pairs or small groups. At this initial stage I ask students not to refer to their exercise books or folders.

Having achieved a complete list I ask students to consider what kind of questions they think would be a good way of assessing their learning, particularly in terms of fairness and being able to understand the questions.

Students are then asked to write two or three questions relating to the topics; to ensure 'coverage' of the terms' work pairs or small groups can be allocated one or two topic areas.

At the end of the lesson I collect all the questions in and decide which ones are going to be the most useful to fit the purpose of the test. I may add some of my own or make changes to the wording of certain questions.

I type up the questions and give the completed test paper to students, whereupon their homework for the final couple of weeks is to revise for the test.

In the test lesson I give students a 'new' copy of the paper and ask them to write their answers on new pieces of paper.